The
English

The

English

DAVID FROST *and* ANTONY JAY

STEIN AND DAY / Publishers / New York

Contents

THE ENGLISH

[6]

Foreword

WHAT has happened to the English? For years they have impressed other nations with their reserve, their effortless superiority, and their massive sense of propriety and responsibility. The bowler-hatted, pinstripe-suited retired colonel with the bristling white moustache served as a satisfactory stereotype; he may not have been universal, he may not even have formed the majority, but it was clear that England was run by him and for him, and that he was the model towards which his less favored compatriots molded their aspirations.

And then suddenly the picture changed. It was not a slow fade, not even a dissolve, but an abrupt cut to a picture of a young man with long hair, very little reserve, and no sense of propriety or responsibility whatever. The mystifying fact, however, was not that he should exist—presumably he existed somewhere even in the old England —but that he suddenly seemed to become the dominant figure, as if he was the one England was run by and run

[7]

for, as if he was the model to which the rest tried to conform. Almost overnight the stately homes of England disappeared from view, and were replaced by the discotheques of swinging London.

The consequence is that the English at the moment are suffering from a severe attack of double image, and it is hard for other nations to know which is a reflection of reality and which is an illusion. Unfortunately it is even harder for most of the English, because this double image is a symptom of deep self-delusion. The assumptions which many Englishmen hold about their country rest on facts which have disappeared since they last looked. The new facts often support exactly the opposite assumption, or one which bears no relationship at all. It is the gap between assumption and evidence, between illusion and reality, that causes the present obscurity both in England and abroad. The authors hope that this book will, by sparking across that gap, provide the necessary flash of illumination for those who want a brief but clear picture of what is really happening to the English.

D. P. F.
A. R. J.

The
English

1

England
Today

THE State of the Nation. It seems to have been the sole pre-occupation of English pundit and Swiss banker alike for some time now. Both appear to have found a picture of unrelieved gloom. Any pundit worthy of the name has found it incumbent upon himself to point out at great length that we are in the depths of a great economic crisis.

In the dear dead days, the pundit recalls, a sports-page headline like DANGEROUS SUSSEX COLLAPSE would send elderly matrons scurrying for the telephone with anguished cries of "Oh dear, I *do* hope my property in Brighton is all right!" But today, alas, even a headline couched in terms as specific and sporting as ENGLAND COLLAPSES BEFORE LUNCH is much more likely to be a quite straightforward account of what has happened to the pound in world markets up until noon. And that, needless to say, isn't cricket at all.

Ruin and misery the pundit sees as he gazes upon his England. Huge debts, inefficient industries, antiquated unions, uncompetitive managements, inadequate exports, depleted reserves, severely restrained wages, congested roads, decaying cities, irresponsible adolescents, irreligious clerics, escaped convicts, television addicts, and short-sighted bureaucrats. All trying to support the crumbling ruins of a derelict empire with an inadequate army, a doubtful currency, and a Royal Mint with a hole in the middle.

Ruin and misery the pundit sees. At the tumbledown center of that derelict empire he sighs, like an exiled monarch in tattered robes, for vanished glories, and weeps his envy of other countries. America for her wealth; Russia for her sense of purpose; France for her independence; Germany for her determination; Japan for her energy. For Swiss banks and Swedish morals. For Caribbean cricketers and Australian tennis players. They curtail their welfare program to placate other countries' bankers, tailor their foreign policy to suit their American creditors, and prepare to abandon their international currency if European neighbors will just let them come in out of the freeze. Only of England's pop singers can our pundit feel proud. And of them he feels, in fact, secretly rather ashamed.

The English, he says, are finished. Lost in apathy. Harrowed with doubt. Tormented with despair. Sackcloth and ashes is their national dress. Bread and water their diet. At least it should be, if his account is true.

Yet if you look around England, what do you see? Full stomachs, smiling faces and a general sense of the mid-day sun. The Englishman is a mad dog still. Expenditure in the shops last Christmas reached an historic peak, which will almost certainly be topped this Christmas. Real estate agents report a strong market for houses over £10,000. Money cascades away on racing and football, and in gambling casinos so lush and busy that they have lured the Las Vegas Mafia to England's green and pleasant land.

England is proud, too, of its export record. It probably exports more scientists and doctors than any other country in the world. More and more people are visiting England's art galleries to see where some of the world's greatest paintings used to hang. England is still the world's leading manufacturer of cricket bats, Union Jacks, sheet music of God Save the Queen, souvenir paperweights of the Tower of London, and second class railway carriages. Carnaby Street, where boy meets girl and doesn't realize it, has made the nation's fashions famous in every corner of the civilized globe. Necklines get lower, hemlines rise. Nobody knows where it is all leading, but everybody wants to be there when it happens. And what is going to happen—what is the reason for all this vivacity and mirth? How to explain that the English, in the midst of all their troubles, are having a grand and glorious time? Is this the last luxurious fling in the once-proud citadel while the Goths are at the gate? Nero fiddling while the Treaty of Rome burns? Is it staggering irresponsibility? The Last Waltz in the flooded first class lounge before the Titanic disappears forever beneath the waves? The tipsy notes of a raucous farewell?

It all seems so out of character. But perhaps the

English character *has* changed utterly in the space of a few years. Is that the explanation? The three most enduring English characteristics, according to foreign observers, have always been hypocrisy, frigidity, and snobbery. Have they disappeared, submerged beneath a tide of honesty, warmth, and friendliness?

Honesty does not seem to have taken over totally from hypocrisy. We talk about our vital links with the Commonwealth, and then cut grants to Commonwealth students. We condemn the color policies of South Africa, Rhodesia, and America, who really have a problem, and congratulate ourselves that by our graceful submission to a West Indian cricket team and the enrolment of one colored policeman we have solved ours; and if we haven't, well, as the man reported in *The Observer* said: "It's all the Queen's fault, anyhow. She goes to all the black countries and they do their war dances for her and they think they can come over here and take our jobs." We talk about redeploying workers when we mean firing them and leaving them to fend for themselves. We ban tobacco advertising on television, which can manage without it, but not in newspapers, which cannot. We permit free speech at Speakers Corner in Hyde Park, which has become the preserve of licensed eccentrics, but arrest and imprison a few students who wave their banners at the Prime Minister in a Brighton church. We create an ombudsman to deal with the errors and omissions of bureaucracy, but deny him the powers he needs to do an effective job. And where do

[14]

you go to complain about an ombudsman? We deplore the rise in illegitimacy while fighting tooth and nail to prevent the Family Planning Association from helping anyone except the married. And books of instruction on more formalized hypocrisy, like knowing how to yawn with your mouth closed, sometimes called etiquette, are consistently best sellers.

Warmth does not seem to have taken over totally from frigidity. A not uncommon experience for a young Englishman is to sit on a sofa with his girl friend in the half darkness while she tells him she has found a shop that sells the most revealing black mini-skirt with slits up the side, really fab, worn with a white see-through skinny sweater that has a hole in the middle and a plunging neckline, and some super fishnet stockings, and a frothy lace petticoat with an op-art silk lining. Inexpressibly intrigued, he attempts to kiss her. And gets his face smacked. The whole business of the sexy young English has been grossly inflated to feed the greedy imagination of an envious older generation. In any case, nobody has ever said the English manage without sex; it has been their incapacity to flirt easily, their uneasiness in the presence of tenderness, that has distinguished them from other nations. And that is unchanged. A sociological team watched, in various countries, how often couples touched each other during conversation. The English came easily at the bottom of the list, as usual. Had Billy Graham realized this—that the English have no unit of erotic currency of lower denomination than

[15]

the full clinch—he would have been less outraged than he was at the scenes he saw on that summer's day in Green Park. Whereas in other countries the standard response, if they even have such a thing, to an introduction is some form of words expressing pleasure and delight, it is still, in England, the most meaningless and chilling conversation-stopper known to humankind: "How d'you do?" The English are as reserved as they ever were, and anyone who doubts it is perfectly welcome to try striking up a conversation with a stranger on a train, but he is advised to take a book on his journey, too. Not even a very interesting book; *Johnson's Guide to Turning and Boring Wood* will prove quite a relief after an English stranger.

Friendliness does not seem to have taken over totally from snobbery. When Mr. George Brown, the Foreign Secretary, goes to a Buckingham Palace banquet in a dinner jacket rather than tails, like the rest of the men; and when the newspapers find this simple fact worthy of attention and comment; and when the English are not merely interested but in some cases actually agitated by it, we surely need no further evidence that England still preserves all the apparatus of a class-ridden society. Both Mr. Brown, by his behavior, and the rest of the population, by theirs, make it perfectly clear that whether or not they approve of class distinctions, they are acutely aware of their existence. What *was* quaint about this little controversy was that nobody was surprised that Mr. Brown, the warm-hearted man who calls everyone "Brother," actually possessed a dinner jacket.

In the factory, there are still the different levels. One man has his lunch in the executive dining room. The second has his lunch in the staff canteen. And the third does not have lunch at all. He brings his dinner with him.

Movement between the classes might be a little easier than it was, but they are still quite separate and any attempt to fuse them meets with resistance and uproar. Nothing, for example, has quite so stirred the English recently as the suggestion that all their children, regardless of class and wealth, should go to the same kind of schools. And nothing has stirred them less than the fact that it was not thought necessary for Prince Charles to pass an entrance examination before being admitted to Cambridge University.

No, the English have not changed. And if anyone is puzzled by their apparently frantic merriment during an apparently desperate national crisis, it can only be because he does not understand that in England nothing it what it appears to be; he does not realize that the English have managed to make Puritanism pleasant and pleasure Puritanical; he has yet to learn that the English are the most peculiar people on God's earth. Their earth.

Puritanism in England has never been an eccentric oddity. It has been in the mainstream of national life for many centuries, and by the beginning of this one, hard work, devotion to duty, and scrupulous attention to every detail of discomfort had secured for John Bull riches beyond the dreams of avarice. He was lord of all he surveyed and much that he had never set eyes on. At this point, he took it into his virtuous head to try a little pleasure; to taste, so to speak, a little drop of gin. It was delicious. John Bull quickly became glossy-cheeked and pot-bellied. And ever since then, the English have been dealing with the dilemma of affluent Puritanism: the problem of how to wear, at one and the same time, a happy smile and a worried frown.

Let anyone who doubts this recall the paroxysms of both distaste and delight into which the whole country was thrown by the Christine Keeler–John Profumo business. The taste for Puritanism was satisfied by hounding Mr. Profumo out of public life and asking a judge, Lord Denning, to look into it and make sure nothing like it ever happened again. Well, nothing *exactly* like it; not too soon. And the taste for pleasure was dealt with by the newspapers, who turned a naïve indiscretion into a saga of passion and intrigue more entertaining and enjoyable than any serial story the English had read since Sir Richard Burton told them his tales of all those Arabian nights. Mr. Mick Jagger learned more recently, however, that even a scandal as luscious as that in the summer of 1963 does not purge the English of the complex of emotions that bred it. They are emotions that merely lie dormant, awaiting the opportunity to revive and break out again.

Our attitude toward any form of corruption or dissipation can be equally severe. The suspicion of drinking is a terrible risk for a politician, and few even today will allow themselves to be photographed with a glass in their hand. Anyone who refuses a drink on a social occasion is usually met with a conspiratorial "Be a devil!" exhortation, as if there were an element of sin about it all. This is a difficult enough state of affairs at any time, but in the midst of our present plenty it is especially agonizing.

Since the English add a voluntary element of discomfort to all of their pleasures, they thus reach an accommodation with their Puritanism. Smokers, happily puffing away, are reminded by posters that they are killing themselves and forced by a penal tax to pay more for their cigarettes than any other addicts in the world. Drinking is restricted to certain hours of the day and just when things are getting really jovial everyone is thrown out of the nice warm pub and made to contemplate their wicked conviviality in the cold street.

Taking someone else's money without his consent is regarded in England, as elsewhere, as sinful, but even their *own* money is thought by the English to be rather filthy and dangerous, so they tuck it away in banks which then refuse, by opening at ten and closing at three, to let them get at it during convenient hours, like just before work in the morning or just after work in the evening. Finally, such of their own money as the English do lay their hands on is not easily spent, since the moment they leave their work in the evening and are free to fling it about, the shops bang down their shutters and only raise them again next morning when everyone is safely back at work.

Three thoroughly uncivilized practices have a special

virtue about them in England, all of them Puritanical: opening windows in cold weather, going for long walks in cold weather, and bathing in cold water. Of course, these practices are so self-evidently unpleasant that none but the most dyed-in-the-wool Englishman actually indulges in them. But every Englishman knows he ought to and if, for example, he gratifies the flesh in a hot bath he immediately afterwards mortifies it with an abrasive towel. And when he knows he should really fling open a window he at least does the next worst thing and lets the fire go low, briskly stamping his feet and rubbing his hands the while, for all the world as though he had just planted the Union Jack at the South Pole. He has learned well the lessons of his childhood. For the more expensive education becomes, the more Puritanical it gets: the warm modern buildings of the primary school, where corporal punishment is forbidden, rise through stages of growing mortification until you reach the damp, drafty, antiquated, unheated buildings, the excessive cramming, uneatable food, and frequent floggings of the really expensive prep school.

Every happiness has its built-in misery. But this alone was not enough to hold back the inexorable tide of affluence. For more than sixty years, John Bull did his best to put off the reckoning. Audit day came slowly, but nonetheless it came. The horrifying moment of full realization was focused by Mr. Harold Macmillan.

Fatefully, unforgettably, he announced it. "You've never had it so good," he said. They were the most dreadful words ever uttered in the English tongue, and it took a Scotsman, with all the clear-eyed contempt they have for the English, to say them. No wonder Macmillan was execrated and never forgiven: he flicked aside for a moment the flimsy veil of misery, transparent to all others, beneath which the English had been accustomed to enjoying themselves. He forced them to face at last the fact that life was really rather fun.

Panic and despair ensued for a while. The personal dilemma which faced every Englishman was that, do what he might, life was good and improving. This in turn produced a national dilemma. For while the English as a nation wanted power and money and international influence, the English as a people were so aghast at all the implications of unabashed affluence that they practically gave up work. Fortunately, a single solution was found for both horns of this dilemma. The government told the people that the nation was in debt. With this one stroke, they penetrated to the very bedrock of Puritanism and drew from the people a gushing new fountain of it. The disgraceful notion of insolvency; the language of squeezes and freezes (such reassuring words); the invocations of Dunkirk and backs-to-the-wall—all these not only enabled the English people to tell themselves they weren't really enjoying themselves at all, but they also gave them good reason to buckle to again.

Another solution would, of course, have been to take over the billions of dollars held overseas by English companies and trusts and give them sterling in exchange at the fair current rate of exchange. When this was publicly proposed, the answer offered was that this would only end the current crisis; *it would not cure the deeper malaise.* The trouble was that it *might* have cured the deeper malaise; it might have confirmed absolutely Mr. Macmillan's horrid words. And that was the last thing the English wanted, people, nation, and government. What they wanted was not a solution but an expiation.

The English felt guilty at their prosperity, yet they wanted it to continue. So they told themselves how awful things were, then, girding themselves again in the wisp of sanctity Mr. Macmillan had so brutally torn, carried on enjoying themselves. They held an election and returned to power by a small margin that party which said most blood-curdlingly, with the dourest non-conformist expressions and in the flattest Puritan accent, that England was ill. Finding its majority too small for business purposes, the Labor government took a closer look at the patient and pronounced it half-dead. They set about the task of building a really vast crisis by instituting a whole series of measures which sounded horribly painful but which did not actually prevent anyone from enjoying himself. Whereupon a grateful and approving nation re-elected the Laborites to office with a hugely-increased majority. The Conservatives wailed woe too late, but it did not take them long to catch the right tone of voice, and soon their admonitions were indistinguishable from Labor's, differing only on how we ought to deal with this terrible state of affairs, neither side daring to risk the electoral extinction of telling us that there was nothing to worry about. This unison was most noticeable over entry into the Common Market. What was the strongest argument the English could find for joining? That it would be like a *cold shower* to their industries. Nothing in the world could be nicer!

So look out, Europe! You may think you have her measure, but beware of England, powered by this new and morally irresistible combination, triumphant Puritanism wedded to virtuous affluence. And above all, remember the lesson that it teaches. With England and the English, the camouflage is good. Things are very rarely what they seem. Very rarely what they seem even to the English.

2

The Classless Society

IT WAS a happy day for England when she began to dismantle her old class system. The divisions into upper, middle, and lower classes had for many decades been the cause of enmity and bitterness that was inimical to the health of the nation and the individuals who comprised it. Snobbery was rife, inequality rampant. The insolence of the upper to the middle class; the vicious indifference of the middle to the lower; the obsequiousness of the lower to both, all in their turn made mock everywhere of ease and good fellowship. Long after all other sensible people had abandoned tiresome notions about good breeding and aristocracy, the English cherished their class structure.

But these are nobler times. The English at last have acknowledged the futility of ancient partitions and swept them away. Mr. Edward Heath takes over from the 14th

Earl of Home; the clubs of St. James's yield to the coffee houses of Chelsea; Carnaby Street usurps Saville Row; Liverpudlian pop stars week-end at ducal castles; dukes go out to work; ancient universities welcome upstart sons of hobnailed workmen. The bad old system is smashed. The archaic pyramid, upper-middle-lower, an unholy trinity of jealousy, malevolence, and frustration, cracks and crumbles. Those at the top—the people who said "looking glass" for mirror, "writing paper" for notepaper, "chimney-piece" for mantelpiece; the people who never said "Cheers" when they drank; the peers and courtiers and country squires—no longer signify. The three great classes melt and mingle. And a new Britain is born.

Classlessness, or the illusion of it, has been created by the process of continuous assimilation through which for centuries England has avoided bloody revolutions and civil disorder and preserved intact its Royal Family and institutions of privilege. Almost everywhere else in the world such traditions succumbed: upper class foreigners fought their class war in one sharp pitched battle, throwing everything they possessed into a contest they were bound to lose (a demonstration of stupidity and vulgarity) which indicates to us that they never really qualified for the term upper class at all, and accounts in large measure for our disdain of foreigners—the English upper classes very wisely avoided trench warfare. Instead, whenever pressure from below grew too strong, they made a tactical withdrawal. Of course, as they withdrew they took with them everything of value which stood upon the territory in dispute, but the territory itself they conceded with good grace and without bloodshed or tears.

For example, when the masses agitated for the vote, they were given it; a vote was then made quite useless by the transfer of power to constituency parties which the upper classes controlled and which chose the candidates for whom the masses, happily enjoying their new liberty, could quite freely cast their ballots. When the middle classes insisted that the Civil Service be released from the private patronage of the swells and made open to entrance by public, competitive examination, their wishes were met at once; the swells withdrew their lucrative sinecures and the victorious middle class found itself in possession of an under-paid, over-worked, much-abused profession. When the population clamored for education, the upper classes swiftly made arrangements to give them an education; that it was inferior to the education the upper classes bought for their own children could scarcely be a matter for criticism since the first lesson the population was taught was that justice, of which their England was the fountainhead and arbiter, required that you get only what you pay for.

What, above all, the upper classes took with them as they walked quietly out of the arena was hostages. They understood perfectly the instincts which led certain people to revolt against the class system, for those instincts were their own. They realized that no rebellion was quite what it seemed to be, or claimed to be, or believed itself to be. They saw that although the majority were childishly delighted with their gains, there were a few—the more thoughtful, the more powerful, the leaders—for whom easy victories against injustice were not enough. The upper classes knew that for some people the very idea that there was a superior class to which they could not belong was so galling and humiliating that they were prepared to do anything to smash it, whatever it gave away. To ferocious, adamant beasts who wanted blood, blue blood, exceptionally soothing treatment was afforded. As they came charging over the horizon, leaving the herd far behind, the castle gates were thrown open wide; and as they stood snorting and quivering with indignation in the tilting yard, they were given exactly what they demanded—blue blood, upper class blood, by the earful.

The leader who arrived first at the gates was eventually the one who asked for the gates to be closed—he couldn't hear what his new friends were saying because of the row from the rabble outside. If the blue bloods played their cards right, he went off eventually to call his children Emma or Phillippa, Hugh, Nigel or Humphrey, quite forgetting the splendid example of the Russians, who announced that in order to promote total classlessness they were giving their children names like "Tractor" and "Industrialization." Nothing more thrills an Englishman, already a member of the superior race, than the discovery that he is moreover a member of the upper class of that race. His innate modesty forbids, of course, that he should himself proclaim it; it's not for him to say he's upper class; all *he* can say is that he's as good as the next man. And if the man next to him happens to be the Prime Minister, or the Lord Chamberlain, or the 28th Duke of Suffolk, or a member of the Royal Family—well, we must draw our own conclusions.

The sturdy conviction of every Englishman that he is as good as the next man has been invaluable both in preserving the upper class and creating an illusion of classlessness. For it enables a man who would once have been called, and called himself, middle or lower class to identify with the man who *used* to be next to him and he believes still is, in spirit.

"Yes, we are all equals now," he can say to himself complacently as he sips his pint of bitter in the local pub and reads in his evening paper that his old friend and former neighbor—"Known him all my life"—has just wrenched his neck playing polo.

It follows from all this that the only people now aware of the distinction between the classes are the upper class; the rest of us are confident the whole thing has been abolished. "I don't have to call *you* 'Sir' do I?" says the party worker to the Cabinet Minister, the waiter to the famous playwright, the train driver to the chairman of a nationalized industry, the gamekeeper to the scrap metal millionaire. "Certainly not, my good man," is the brisk reply; and any vague feeling of uncertainty it might arouse is soon assuaged. "After all," he tells himself, "I *am* a good man; good as he is any day, even if I don't play polo." Then he goes off for a nice game of darts.

It follows, too, that far from being narrow and exclusive, the upper class is an expanding one. It has had to countenance the inclusion of a whole new elite minority in order to maintain the exclusion of the majority. Besides those born into it, it is ready to include, if necessary kidnap, anyone who fulfills three prime qualifications. First, obviously, you must show that you are aware of the existence of an upper class and an upper class way of life. Second, you must have a clearly defined attitude to it; approving or disapproving matters not but half measures will not do. Third, you must be seen to be either very, very diligent and generous in supporting the upper class, or dangerously purposeful in undermining it. Given these characteristics, you are very quickly accepted, or conscripted, as a probationary member. Full membership follows a few lessons in realism and one or two trifling adjustments of your attitude. Whatever it *was,* you are taught, it must henceforth be muted. You must not draw attention to your new class. Just pretend, like everyone else, that it does not exist. Probationary members, by the way, are easily identified by the careful listener. Shakespeare has told us how:

"Lowliness is young ambition's ladder,
   Whereto the climber upward turns his face.

[30]

But when he once attains the upmost round
He then unto the ladder turns his back,
Looks in the clouds, scorning the base degrees
By which he did ascend. . . ."

As soon as you hear someone scorning the base degrees by
which he did ascend, using phrases like "the average con-
sumer," "the mass audience," "the common man" and "the
man in the street" in a way which clearly excludes himself,
you can be sure you are listening to a probationary upper
classer who has had his attitude adjusted but has not yet
had his voice lowered.

Broadly speaking, what is financially required of the
new recruit is a bank balance and an attitude of mind
which can be in inverse proportion. If you have been
brought up with the right attitude of mind, you do not
need the big bank balance. If you have not, you probably
do. Conversely if you have a big bank balance, it becomes
fairly easy to acquire the attitude of mind.

How does England's new classless class system work?
We have seen how it survives, but how does it operate?
What actually happens in the "new" system? Consider this
report in an English newspaper: "Princess Margaret
traveled last night to Balmoral as an ordinary first class
passenger in the Aberdonian night train out of King's
Cross." Now, this is just the sort of thing that convinces
foreigners that the English are a quiet, unexceptional
people. But why, if nothing exceptional was happening,

was it thought worth reporting at all? Why bother with the fact that Princess Margaret got on a train going to Scotland, something hundreds of other English people did that night? And of course the answer is that Princess Margaret, whatever she may feel about it personally, is a representative of the pinnacle—the Royal Family—of the class system we are discussing. The fact that that system exists is smoothly glossed over by describing her as "an ordinary first class passenger." But it is as difficult to talk about ordinary first class passengers as it would be to discuss your average common-or-garden, man-in-the-street Pope.

Princess Margaret did not travel as an ordinary passenger at all. Apart from anything else, no ordinary passenger, first or second, gets her name in the paper simply because she has boarded a train. Princess Margaret cannot go anywhere or do anything as an ordinary person, however hard she tries, for the simple reason that she is *not* an ordinary person or passenger. She is a very extraordinary person. As extraordinary, in the English class sense, as every other member of the Royal Family. And this fact is illustrated in the next sentence of the report: "As the train drew out, fellow-passenger Rhoda Williamson said, 'I had no idea the Princess would be on the Aberdonian. I'm so excited I shan't get a wink of sleep.'"

Two makes of motor car, Jaguars and Minis, give a special insight into class attitudes. One of the class rules is that if you are upper class you should not rub it in; another is that if you are in the lower class you should not show you are trying to get into the upper. Now, both Jaguars and Minis were designed straightforwardly as good motor cars. But because they are good without reference or concession to the class system—unlike, for example, Rolls Royces and Ford Populars—most people, upper and lower, are worried by them. They have no objection to a Ford Popular, but are afraid of a Mini; the upper class because they suspect the owner is trying to ape them, who use Minis as *second* cars; the lower because they suspect the owner is as nippy, maneuverable and intrusive as the car he is driving: it seems always to get to the head of the line at traffic lights.

Consider education. The English educational system is only secondarily an apparatus for educating children. It is primarily a skirmishing ground over which our children fight the preliminary rounds of the class battle in which some of them will take more serious part when they grow up. In so many cases have the preliminaries, known as eleven-plus examinations,* been decisive that a huge uproar broke out about them a year or two ago. English parents have little knowledge of, or interest in, the content and methods of the teaching their children receive, and if the eleven-plus had been anything to do with that, it

---

* Taken by English children shortly before their eleventh birthday, this exam determines the kind of further education they will get—either academic or vocational.

would have caused no more concern than the annual chest X-ray. But it was not. It was a test to decide whether a child should remain lower class or have a chance of becoming upper. It had an explosive effect not because such a test was itself thought reprehensible but because it was being given at too early an age. Failure at the age of eleven meant that a child could not go to one of the grammar schools which are, or were, the great processing plants that take masses of lower class children in at one end and, at the other, turn out a sprinkling of potential upper class children along with a slightly reduced mass of lower class.

The upper class, with its customary grace and good sense, has conceded all the disputed territory, and carried the valuables over the horizon. The eleven plus has been abolished; the grammar schools are threatened with extinction. Our children will be given a classless education, in comprehensive schools. Not until their early teens will they now encounter, in the shape of university entrance examinations, the upper-lower selective process.

To some people, even this concession was repellent and unworthy. A writer in the *Yorkshire Evening Press* said: "Before long we shall have the children so educated that there will be no one available for sweeping the roads and doing the vitally necessary but less remunerative jobs. Get the children out to work at fourteen (you will have fewer delinquents) and only those with academic qualities should stay on for further education."

Get them out to work. Well, if there is one area in which the upper class has shown it knows how to take care of itself it is in industry. Our mills, mines, shipyards and so on were founded by upper class families and staffed by anyone who needed a crust of bread. There were the owners (gentlemen) and the workers (not gentlemen). The owner-family worked in carpeted rooms while the workers toiled on cold concrete floors; the family ate in the boardroom while the workers wolfed their sandwiches at the bench; the family continued to draw its dividends when the workers were laid off. After many years of this, some of the workers felt so insulted and humiliated that they began to agitate for change, not merely for themselves but for their fellow-workers, too. The family were most helpful. They gave such people some sort of less tiring work with pens and ledgers and a little more time to eat their sandwiches.

The agitation subsided, only to break out again a couple of decades ago. This time, the upper class (no longer entirely family, of course) went whole hog and took the leaders of the lower class entirely to their bosom. Now, those leaders have air-conditioned, carpeted offices, while the workers toil on the concrete floor or at their ranges of desks; they eat in elegant dining rooms or expensive restaurants, while the workers line up in cafeterias or canteens; they still draw their pay, monthly, when the workers are laid off, or re-deployed. And they will never again agitate for change. They are known, collectively, as

[35]

management. And they are on the way to upper class. If meanwhile the shop assistants wish—as they did in Bridlington—to call themselves "retail tacticians" or "counter public relations officers," then let them. For everything that conceals the true nature of the division between the different levels can only be advantageous. For the reality of the situation is the reality of the Turkish proverb: "If a stone falls on an egg, alas for the egg. If an egg falls on a stone, alas for the egg."

The way an Englishman actually uses the vote the upper class gave him years ago does not necessarily indicate his class. He may be upper class, yet vote Socialist; lower, yet vote Conservative. A much clearer sign is given by what party he joins and works for, and the reason the Young Conservatives are so much stronger than the Young Socialists is that they represent a route from the lower to the upper class. If your parents are upper class and you are rebelling against *them*, though not against their class, you join the Young Socialists, which is why they are such an undisciplined and unruly lot. The Liberal Party is a device to enable older non-graduates to vote against the Conservatives without any fear that they are leaving the upper class.

Anyone who says he is Labor is definitely lower class, but he who calls himself Socialist might be upper or lower. Similarly, anyone who calls himself a Conservative invites close inspection, whereas the man who says he is a Tory is almost definitely upper class.

THE CLASSLESS SOCIETY

Doubts as to the category of a Socialist or a Conservative can often be resolved by observing a man's attitudes toward sex and sex talk, since fashion in taboo subjects takes longer than any others to seep down from the upper to the lower class. Your upper class man has a permissive attitude toward sex, toward intellectual sex talk, and toward four letter words when they mean what they say. A lower class man uses four letter words only for swearing, and then only in confined, man-to-man situations; he is repelled by sex talk unless it is in the form of dirty jokes; and he regards sex in general as an extremely personal domain about which his wife, but certainly nobody else, might, at a pinch, venture an elliptical remark. He is easily offended and shocked; matter which would cause a catastrophic drop in the circulation of his newspapers and magazines can be published without a second thought in those read by the upper class. It is noteworthy that the first Englishman to use the dreaded four letter word on television was a first generation upper class Socialist, and he used it with exquisite, literal precision. Upper class viewers hardly noticed; the lower class was absolutely appalled. Not once before had the word escaped the lips of their television representatives, though they had had thousands of opportunities to use it when they were being interviewed in news and documentary programs about hardships and misfortunes to which, in its various forms as an epithet, it could so well have been applied.

There is not a great deal else in their talk to distinguish one class from another now that the upper class, to help the illusion of classlessness, makes such frequent use of lower class locution and accent, but one or two typical phrases are useful distinguishing marks. At a party, "Do you know our hostess?" means an upper class person is delicately trying to find a kindred soul to talk to. "I'm sure *you* know our hostess," means he now realizes he has mistakenly accepted an invitation to a lower class party. "What a sweet house you have," means what a small house. "What an interesting house," is an ugly house. "What a splendid house," describes an ostentatious house. All three are terms used by the upper class, who imagine (wrongly but it doesn't matter) that the lower class is as obsessed as they by architecture and interior decoration. "This is uncle George—he's the *amusing* one in the family," means that uncle George is so vulgar he is quite likely to belch in your face and his aspiring relatives hope you won't hold it against them.

In today's apparently classless England, an apparently classless woman can write in an apparently classless newspaper, *The Observer:* "I was eating a moussaka in Bolton the other day which (though nice) was made with potato, and it suddenly made me realize just how little you can take aubergines for granted out of town."

Well, no, you can't take *anything* for granted in England now. The Duke of Marlborough would confirm that. Leaving his valet behind at Blenheim Palace, he went to stay recently as a guest in someone else's house. His hostess was surprised to hear him complain that his tooth-brush "did not foam properly," so would she get him a new one. He had to be told, gently, that without the aid of tooth paste or tooth powder, usually applied for him each morning by his valet, even a new toothbrush would not foam properly.

The Duke of Roxburghe would confirm it, too. When the Labor Parliamentary candidate in the last election called at his place, Floors Castle, to solicit his vote, he was told by the butler, "You must use the tradesman's entrance." As the College of Arms once told an anxious hostess who sought its advice over the seating arrangements for her dinner party: "The Aga Khan is held to be a direct descendant of God. . . . An English Duke takes precedence."

But why is it that the English have only tinkered with their class system and not, like the rest of the apparently civilized world, completely abandoned it? It is surely very curious that an Englishman petitioning for divorce on the grounds of cruelty can still claim without being laughed out of court that he was "woken in the middle of the night by his wife hitting him on the head and screaming awful abuse, including a statement that he was born and bred in Clapham."

First of all, it is very comfortable to have a class system. Once you establish yourself in the upper class, trivial accidents like a drop in income cannot dislodge you so long as you keep the right attitude. Whereas Americans, for example, have to keep on working harder to keep their income up in order to stay in their social group, an upper class Englishman doesn't have to bother. Once he is in, he can relax. His place in the upper class is secured by what he is, not by what he does. He can be as inefficient as he likes, so long as he is inefficient from the right point of view. The point of view so aptly expressed by a trade union leader who, interviewed in *The Guardian,* denied the charge that trade union leaders were out of touch with the rank and file. He said it was the rank and file who were out of touch with the leadership.

The system is a perfect consolation for failure. The failures in the upper class have the consequences cushioned by the fact that they remain in the upper class even if they are destitute. Institutions like "The Distressed Gentlefolk's Aid Association" show by their very existence that even if you are flat broke you still belong to the upper class and that there is very little, if anything, that can take that away from you.

The system is a perfect let-out for failures in the lower class, too. Instead of being forced to try harder they can tell themselves that their lack of success is due to the system. Card games have always been popular in England, whereas chess has not, for the simple reason that if you lose you can always say you were dealt a lousy hand. In short, the system is a powerful buttress to that great English quality, the uncompetitive spirit.

Clearly, the English preserve their class system because

they want it. If it really was against the Englishman's instinct, he would have got rid of management dining rooms and first class compartments long ago. But the English are a race of snobs and suddenly the game is wide open: there are more opportunities than ever before of being promoted to the upper class. But what of all those losers? Those members of the lower class who have failed all the entrance exams—failed the eleven plus, couldn't face joining the Young Conservatives, haven't made a pile of money, haven't made it to management level, still like their fish and chips. Less docile and oppressed than their forefathers, might they not revolt in numbers too large for the upper class to assimilate?

They will not. Because they are English, and therefore suffused with the essence of snobbery—which is to feel in your heart that there is at least *one* layer below you; one group you can regard as your inferior.

A group lower than the low has, necessarily, to be an outcast group; quite beyond the pale. And for centuries the snobbery of a lower class Englishman was sustained and nourished by the fact that all over the world, throughout his glorious Empire, there were fellow-citizens of his who would bend the knee because he was white, then bend the head because he was English. He was superior to someone. And he was content.

The Empire crumbled. And there were, indeed, faint sounds of revolution as the lower class realized uneasily that they were now truly at the bottom of the heap. Then there began to arrive, in hundreds of thousands, people they could look down on in their very own country. These newcomers took up the most menial jobs; they lived in the very worst houses. They were even a different color, so that nobody, nobody at all, could mistake one of our lower class for one of them. Already they receive the indiscriminate abuse traditionally reserved for the no-class outcast—dirty, lazy, unhygienic, insolent (which means behaving as though there was no such thing as a different class) and before long they will suffer the final condemnation. They will be accused, if they manage to get a bath, of keeping coal in it.

And so the Empire, that much-abused institution, performs its last and its greatest service for the Mother Country. From Trinidad and Barbados, from India and Africa, it sends its sons to save the class system.

3

The Law Unto Itself

FOR anyone who wishes to know and understand the English a study of their system of law and of their criminal activities is essential. The two matters are, of course, closely related, but not perhaps in the way they are related in other countries. The general view of English crime has been dominated since 1964 by the £2½ million Great Train Robbery. But, since it has always been understood that if the English put their minds seriously to anything, including banditry, they will *invariably* come up with something quite staggering, this is not a good case on which to base any conclusions about the English attitude to the law and the way it works. It is better to approach the matter through a crime widely practiced, widely enjoyed and widely deplored. Something everyone the whole world over can easily comprehend. The crime of being drunk and disorderly.

[43]

Let us take a little case of drunkenness reported in the *Woking Herald*. The magistrates were told that the strongest evidence against the defendant was that when he was being examined and put through various tests to see if he was drunk, he was asked to clench his teeth, "whereupon, he took them out, gave them to the divisional surgeon and said 'here, you clench them.'"

Now, most people would say that any man who dared to make such an outrageously provocative remark, in a police station, to a police surgeon, must, absolutely *must* be either a foolhardy drunk or a dangerous revolutionary. In any other country in the world "Here, you clench them" would be overwhelming evidence against the defendant. An open and shut case.

Not, however, in England. It was a witty remark, perhaps. Bold certainly. But evidence that a man was drunk? Not at all. An Englishman is permitted such liberties. Nevertheless, the defendant *was* found guilty. Because he did something the English judiciary cannot imagine any sober Englishman would do. Something so outrageously provocative that he must, absolutely *must* have been drunk. He deliberately proclaimed, by taking his false teeth out in public, that he was lower class.

Let there be no misunderstanding. It is not a criminal offense to be lower class. But it is an assumption of English law that crime is committed by the lower classes, and if evidence can be brought to show that the defendant is lower class, then the prosecution has three-quarters proved its case. In this particular case, as the prosecutor drily remarked, the defendant convicted himself out of his own mouth.

Take another case, this time of stealing. The defendant was said to have been seen leaving a butcher's shop with six chickens in his basket. He had not paid for them. Well, he could have put up several defenses to that apparently compromising situation. Perhaps the best would have been that he was having a big dinner party that evening and that, since he never bothered to carry cash with him, he had intended to send the butcher an explanatory note and a check. Or he might have claimed that the butcher was a scurvy knave who had sold him some indifferent tournedos the day before and he had taken the chickens to teach the butcher a lesson. He could have said he was an exceptionally devout vegetarian who was doing what little he could to prevent other people from eating meat.

Defenses of this sort would not necessarily have succeeded, but at least they would have been sufficiently ambiguous, in class terms, to have left him room for maneuver. What he actually said was, "I'd had a row with the wife and I was taking the chickens home to throw at her." This immediately revealed to the court that he was lower class, and was therefore to be dealt with on the basis that he was likely to be a criminal; certainly he was someone to be watched carefully and treated strictly. It was not, of course, the content of what he said that betrayed him. Indeed an upper-class Englishman could have submitted exactly the same explanation and stood a good chance of being acquitted. The fact that the defendant and his wife had quarreled meant nothing—couples of every degree do that. And that he proposed to bombard her with chickens was, *prima facie,* no more than eccentric. It was the *way* he expressed himself that was his undoing. For he called his wife "*the* wife" a usage that the upper class, which includes the whole higher apparatus of the law, never permits itself.

A broad definition of crime in England is that it is any lower-class activity which is displeasing to the upper class. Crime is committed by the lower class and punished by the upper class, and the whole paraphernalia of the criminal law and the criminal courts is based on the need of the upper class to keep the lower class in its place. Hence the phrase "the criminal class." That is who it refers to. This was unthinkingly admitted by the senior policeman who, reporting on a junior detective, said that the young man was not suited to crime work in Mayfair, "but was in his element in dealing with the lower class criminal operating in Soho." The implication was that there is a distinction between upper-class and lower-class crime. And so there is. Children of the upper classes are made wards of court. Those of the lower classes are hauled before the juvenile courts in need of care and protection. The upper classes sue each other for libel. The lower classes smite each other in public houses and are charged with causing an affray. The upper classes get divorces. The lower classes get five years for bigamy. If a lower class man pins somebody against a brick wall and beats the living daylights out of him, it's called assault and battery. If an upper class man does it, it's called the Eton Wall Game.

One only has to visit a few courts and hear the suave, confident, upper-class accents of Bench and Bar, and the hesitant, ungrammatical, regional accents of the dock, to appreciate that the most important function of our courts is to teach the lower class a lesson. Thus a millionaire with a north country accent is perfectly acceptable—except as a judge. When, during the trial of a man accused of murdering his wife, their lodger, a retired colonial administrator, said in his evidence that he heard a shot but did not leave his apartment because, "I assumed the woman was being assaulted and I had no wish to get involved," the court understood perfectly. They would not get involved either were it not for the necessity of dealing with the extravagances of a lower class lodging-house keeper and his woman.

The breeding, education, training, and working lives of the people who control our courts—most of them elderly males in fancy dress—seem to be specially designed to isolate them from the pressures and emotions and realities which have shaped and conditioned the lives of nine tenths of the people who come before them. Their assumptions about life are grotesque. They are sometimes spectacularly out of touch. Not just the occasional "Who, pray, are the Beatles?" "I understand they are a modern choral society, m'lud." But prosecuting counsel in the case brought against the publishers of *Lady Chatterley's Lover* asking the jury the classic question—was it the sort of book they would let "their servants" read? Or Lord Mansfield Lord Lieutenant of Perthshire remarking "I would like to see offenders finding things a lot less comfortable. I would like to see things like the treadmill introduced again." We can be sure he did not, when he spoke, have in mind hundreds of aristocrats plodding their weary way around the mighty wheel.

It is the lower classes for whom things should be made a lot less comfortable. Sometimes they save the courts the bother by making things uncomfortable for themselves. As the Essex magistrate said, dismissing a charge of assault brought by a woman against her husband: "It is not unreasonable, in a certain class, for a woman to have her face smacked from time to time, and to be punched about. It is the normal wear and tear of their married life." Or the incredulous judge at Leicester: "Surely you cannot expect the court to believe that. Is it not plain that if there is one thing a reasonable man does not want after eating his Sunday dinner it is to have his feet tickled?" Not, certainly, in his lordship's house. Or any other upper-class house. But the lower classes, to the astonishment and dismay of the upper, take their pleasures as they come along. And the judges have to try and put matters right. "It is my duty, young man, to teach you to mend your ways. Ninety-nine years."

This is what has to be remembered about the law: beneath that cold, harsh, impersonal exterior there beats a cold, harsh, impersonal heart. Like absentee landlords, judges and lawyers draw their livelihood from fields of experience they have never seen, fields that are tilled by people whose emotions they can never share. If they *could* share—or at least understand—their work would be impossible. That is why they turn it all into a play, with a stage, a stage management staff and a cast in period costume. Like all members of England's learned professions, they have the great advantage that only they can make the rules about how their profession shall be conducted and practiced. Tradespeople are hemmed in by Board of Trade inspectors and a host of laws and by-laws drawn up by non-tradespeople. If they offend in the practice of their trade, they will be brought before a court. And it would be very surprising if a delinquent grocer, let's say, were tried by a court consisting solely of grocers. Yet that is the way the professions are run. A doctor, for example, is bound and controlled in the practice of his profession—except for extreme wickedness or folly—only by a set of rules drawn up by his fellow doctors, all of whom recognize that a doctor has to make a good upper-class living. A lawyer is in an even better position. Not only do lawyers have the same advantages as doctors, in drafting the code that regulates their own behavior; they also draft the laws which we all have to obey. It is as though they were doctors, with the additional privilege of inventing all the diseases.

This is of particular significance in civil law, the area of activity that makes lawyers rich. They have so arranged things that the more money there is involved in a lawsuit the higher are the legal costs. One suit over an estate of £2½ million resulted in a legal bill of £100,000. We can be quite sure that if the estate had been worth only £2½ thousand there would have been far fewer legal complexities, since there would have been far smaller legal pickings. That legal charges increase in proportion, not to the amount of legal work apparently involved but to the amount of money available for their payment, is shown very clearly by the professional rule that the legal charges for arranging the purchase of a house *must* increase with the cost of the house. The English understand that there can be no question, if they want some legal work done, of getting estimates from three or four different lawyers, as they would get estimates from three or four different builders and decorators if they wanted a room painted. We know we cannot treat our lawyers like our grocers. We can *tell* the television repair man that the shop around the corner does the job cheaper, but we cannot say a comparable thing to our lawyers. First, because the legal shop around the corner would *not* do it cheaper, and second, because we all know we are dealing with people from the upper class. And what they say goes. As a judge said to a witness who took the oath with one hand in his pocket, "Just remember, my man, that you are addressing the Almighty, and a High Court judge."

Although England's laws are designed on the whole to protect the upper class and catch out the delinquent lower, the mesh of the net cannot be so precise that it never catches anyone from the upper class. But if the same law catches the upper class too often, then the law is changed. The laws restraining homosexuality, for example, were framed for the criminal lower classes, and a great deal of the aristocratic ill-feeling directed against Oscar Wilde was due to the fact that he had betrayed the upper class by showing that it, too, sometimes behaved naughtily. After his time, more and more upper class people were convicted of homosexual offenses. Much larger numbers of lower class people were convicted too, yet pressure to change the law came not from their ranks, but from those above. And we now have the situation where Treasury Counsel can say of a charge of indecency laid against a well-known gentleman, "It is a perfectly ordinary little case of a man charged with indecency with four or five guardsmen."

It is not the fundamental justice or injustice of the law that worries the upper class. It is the fact that, if they are not very careful, "quite nice" people might have to go to jail. When the law itself cannot be changed; when it is absolutely certain to catch a certain number of upper class people, then the law—which, as Anatole

THE ENGLISH

France said, "with magnificent impartiality forbids rich
and poor alike to steal bread and sleep under bridges"—
devises alternative punishments. Traffic laws, for example,
catch a lot of upper class people. So offenders are offered
the option of paying a fine or going to prison. The upper
class pay fines, which do not bother them at all; the lower
class beg, borrow, and scrape the money together as best
they can, or go to jail, where they belong. Nobody wants
literate people to go to prison—they have a distressing
way of revealing what it's actually like and destroying our
illusions about training and rehabilitation with nasty
stories about sadism and futility and buckets of stale urine.
Anyway there is no need to send the upper classes to
prison. Anything that can be done for them by prolonged,
enforced separation from their families, in an all-male,
highly disciplined and regimented society employed in
futile occupations, has already been achieved at their public
schools. It is hardly surprising if judges who have been
to Eton and Winchester have few qualms about sending
lower class young men to Parkhurst or Wormwood Scrubs.

The question is: why are there so many young men
at the moment qualifying to be sent to Parkhurst or
Wormwood Scrubs? After all, crime is not exactly a new
phenomenon. The first law given to man was that he
should not eat the fruit of the tree of knowledge, and we
all know how long it took for Adam and Eve to break it.
Crime has been running in the human family ever since.
All the same, it is commonly suggested nowadays that

[52]

crime springs either from some character defect or from poverty and need. The London of Oliver Twist is the stereotype of a crime-prone community. This might be true of other countries, but it is not true in England today. If it were, then our growing understanding of mental illness and its treatment, and our steadily rising affluence should be making the crime figures drop year by year until it reached a hard core of children and middle-aged housewives shoplifting, and a few disturbed personalities and sick minds. Instead, crime is growing to proportions it never reached in the darkest days of urban poverty and squalor in the nineteenth century. As the level of affluence has risen, so has the level of crime. We can scarcely open our papers or switch on the television news without hearing of a new jewel robbery or attack on a bank. The upper class law makers can barely keep up with the lower class law breakers, so few of whom seem to have been brought up like little Leslie Hargraves who, according to the *Daily Herald* a few years ago, was taken by his mother to stand outside Wandsworth prison on the morning that a man was to be hanged for murder. The *Herald* reported: "It was the second time Leslie had stood among execution 'watchers.' 'He'll never forget it,' said his mother. 'He'll keep asking questions. And when he grows up, he'll know the difference between right and wrong.'"

To the chagrin of the upper class, this is a difference most of us never seem to get into our heads. What is there, they ask themselves, about the society they have organized for us that makes so many turn against it and cut themselves off from it? Of course there is the professional criminal, and the man who just cannot cope and scarcely knows what he is doing. But what of all the rest? We have work, security, a health service, a full range of welfare services; surely it's enough to keep us from crime? Surely our rising crime figures cannot be accounted for by an increasing number of needy people? Are not the two worlds Disraeli spoke of coming together faster than ever before?

Yes, they are, in the sense that there is no longer an army of have-nots and a small group of haves. Nevertheless, the rich and the poor are as far apart as ever; it is just less obvious because it is no longer money that really divides them. The two worlds are built into English life from the very start. By the division between secondary modern school and grammar school. The real difference is the difference between interest and boredom, between aspiration and resignation. It was well-expressed by the youth caught firing an airgun at windows. "What else is there to do in Barnstaple on a Sunday?" he asked the Devonshire magistrates.

The boy who leaves a secondary modern school— or a comprehensive, it makes virtually no difference—at fifteen enters a totally different world from his contemporary who goes on to take his O levels—examinations important to getting into college, or into a good white-collar job. For the O level boy, there are all sorts of hopes and possibilities. He may not realize them all, he may not get very high, but he knows that there are responsible jobs around which need filling; jobs for supervisors and under-managers and so on, which are open to him once he has his precious certificates. And if he has A level, or a degree, there are even more attractive and promising avenues open to him.

But seventy per cent of the population leave school at fifteen. And for the majority of *them,* the outlook is very different. Quite simply, they face a dead end. They go into the factory and are shown their place at the bench, with the knowledge that they are more or less bound to stay there until they retire at sixty or sixty-five. They can look around the factory and see men of their father's generation, perhaps even their grandfather's, doing just about the same work as themselves, for just a fraction more pay because of their seniority in meniality. It may sound like a caricature, but for an enormous number of school leavers it is the literal truth. The idea of a job's being fun, or satisfying, or challenging, is only for a privileged minority. Even the idea of progress is non-existent. The boy who goes into a factory after leaving school at fifteen does not think in terms of promotion; of becoming a fore-man, or a supervisor. He knows that there is no route up any ladder for the likes of him. The only way for a lower class boy to break through is by climbing up the academic ladder. If he is not academic, he might as well give up trying. He is stuck at his bench for good.

He finds, moreover, that the world he has gone out into is totally organized, not only at work, but everywhere else, too. There has never been so much running of things, so much governing; or in his case, being governed. Not just by the firm he works for, with all its labor policies and inspectors and supervisors and personnel officers and foremen and managers and union officials and shop stewards. Not just by the laws of the land, enforced by policemen. There are also rent collectors and insurance men and installment collectors and council inspectors and health visitors and welfare officers and a host of other people, all of whom represent authority in one form or another; all of whom can make him do this, or stop doing that, or ask him for information about the other. All of them instruments of a society that is incredibly highly organized and governed (which is not the same as incredibly well organized and governed). He finds that he has practically no control over his own environment. He exists in order to be governed.

Of course, he can learn to accept this, and most people do. They recognize that the job is just a great slab of tedium which is going to take up most of the middle part of their lives. But, with good fellowship within it, with a growing family, and with the faint hope of hitting the jackpot in the football pools, life can be tolerable, even enjoyable if you have the right temperament. One such cheerful chap wrote to the *Daily Telegraph*: "I have a wife, a television, a fridge and a washing machine. I have all I want in life."

THE LAW UNTO ITSELF

But suppose you have not got the temperament? Where do you find the challenge, the excitement, the stretching of your capabilities, the test of your courage and nerve that some people need to make them feel that they are living and not just existing? There was a time when the simple business of staying alive and getting food and shelter for a family was enough of an achievement in itself; but not any more. There was a time when you could enlist as a soldier and fight wars; but not any more. There was a time when you could go out to a colony, open up the west, pioneer new frontiers; but not any more. And it's no good trying to start a revolution. For one thing, most people are happy enough with their present situation, and for another, the arms of government and organization are so long and so far reaching that, even allowing for the normal level of incompetence, they would still find out what you were up to before you had a chance to get the thing going.

In spite of the fact that you were turned out of school at fifteen because you showed little academic skill, you may have a lot of drive, good organizing ability, the gift of leadership, nerves of steel and the courage of a lion. But because you are mystified by simultaneous equations or adverbial clauses, there is no organized route for you to take within the framework of English society. That society ordains that you are and will remain lower class.

Suppose, then, that you step outside the framework. Suppose you ignore all the laws and by-laws and regulations and instructions; all the commissioners and council officials and clerks. Suppose, above all, you ignore your class situation, and decide to operate in your own interest, and your own interest alone. Then your skills can have full play. You can recruit a body of men, give them tasks and functions and responsibilities. You can make complicated and elaborate plans, plot a coup which demands courage and daring and complete secrecy and total acceptance of your orders and your authority. In fact, you take your place among the organizers and governors even though it is on the other side of the blanket.

If you had gone to grammar school and taken your A levels, none of that would have been necessary. There would have been no dead end job for you. While your secondary school contemporary was planning the robbery, you would be planning a new public works project or organizing the building of a hydro-electric dam in Africa. You would be getting somewhere and doing something with your life.

Of course not every crime or criminal is motivated by ambitions as deeply felt as this. But is it surprising that for many people who contemplate a small crime or a large one, a small stroke that is against the law or a bold one, the immediate feelings of frustration they have experienced at first hand are stronger than the pep talks about law and order which they can scarcely remember? Never before have people been so well informed about what they are missing. Is it really surprising that crime is on the increase? Already, the big corporations have found that the police cannot possibly cope with their needs and have recruited their own police forces in Security Express, Securicor and the like. We will soon be in the position which obtained in the most lawless days of the nineteenth century, when rich householders in expensive residential districts also recruited their own police to guard their precincts. Indeed, many of the rich and powerful are suggesting a return to nineteenth century methods of dealing with criminals, particularly the worst ones.

"For murderings of policemen, prison officers, security men, and for murderings for robbery, I would suggest amputations of both legs up to the body, plus prison for ten years, with no artificial limbs ever in the offing. Only a small cart on very small wheels. Further violence, if any, could be dealt with by further deformities," as one of them wrote in the *Huddersfield Daily Examiner*. At the other end of the scale, we have this sort of suggestion, in the *Daily Mail*: "Hooliganism among teenage boys could be restrained if mothers kept them in boy's clothes until the late teens. Short trousers keep a boy from getting big ideas."

The real trouble is that a good half of the law-abiding section of society is not quite sure which side it is on. A far larger number than those who actually take up crime feel a resentment at the number of ways in which they are organized and restricted and dragooned and investigated by all the various authorities. They cannot help feeling a kind of admiration for those who defy the most powerful administration of that authority. It is certain that more people were delighted than distressed by the

Great Train Robbery and, in spite of the fact that the train driver was bludgeoned, they were sorry for the ones who were caught and sentenced, even though they would never themselves have dreamed of taking part in such an enterprise. It is the inclination of the English to side with the underdog, for the simple reason that most Englishmen are themselves underdogs, baffled, bamboozled and ordered about by overdogs.

What—apart from the unthinkable, the abolition of our class system—is the solution? How can we reduce the crime figures? Perhaps the answer to this problem lies in television. The *Daily Mirror* has reported the case of a woman who said: "Three of my children went to approved schools for minor offences. Another was beginning to go the same way until I got a television set on an installment plan. The boy became as good as gold. He started to go to church after watching services on television, and would not go out even when we wanted him to. Since the set went back because of non-payments, he has reverted to his old ways."

It might be too late to save that lad, but perhaps something can still be done for the rest of us. There are about twenty crime thrillers a week on our television screens. And in all of them, authority invariably triumphs. No wonder we are all subconsciously hoping that real life will vary the pattern! No wonder we hope the poor, downtrodden criminal will get away with it!

If the upper class wants our support in combating the

crime wave; if (which is doubtful), all judges and lawyers want to be put out of work, they should use their authority to arrange for a week of wholesale butchery on the telly. Steed, Barlow, Gideon, John Drake, The Saint, Jack Warner, and Lockhart, not to mention Batman and Robin —all must be hideously done to death by the crooks before our very eyes. If only, for one moment, authority and the upper classes would consent to become the underdogs, then the criminals would not have a hope. They would be facing a nation in arms until the crime wave had shrunk to an undetectable ripple.

4

Getting
Around

IN 1841, when Thomas Cook took his first outing of 574
passengers from Leicester to Loughborough, twelve miles
away, eighty per cent of the travelers had never been
outside Leicester in their lives. This may seem surprising
now, but it certainly wasn't then. After all, what business
had the common people to be traveling? To market and
back was the greatest distance they ever needed to go,
and in most cases it was the greatest distance they ever
went. Travel of any greater distance was for important
people or their representatives and had been for centuries.
The King and his court, judges on circuits, tax gatherers,
church dignitaries, rich merchants and traders, noblemen
and squires traveling to London for Parliament—these
were the only people you expected to find any farther
than a day's walk from their homes. Anyone else would
probably be a wandering friar, a vagabond, a highwayman
or thief. Of course, by Thomas Cook's time there was
rather more travel than that going on, but it is clear that

even in his day it was not a form of activity for common people. The middle classes went about on business fairly frequently, the gentry traveled to meet each other in their homes, and many more officials were traveling on government business, but travel of any distance was still fairly conclusive proof of status and importance.

The steam engine, and later the internal combustion engine, put an end to all that. But, although the machines made travel possible for everyone, they could not so easily put an end to the attitudes and prejudices of centuries. The idea of travel being intimately connected with authority and wealth and privilege remained; and it is still enshrined in England's travel system and travel thinking. The general theory is still that the farther you are going, the more important you are. Air and sea travel and long distance train travel carry the most kudos, and those who make these journeys are treated with appropriate deference.

Unfortunately, there is no way of keeping the common people out of it. Indeed, without them the whole system would be uneconomic. So the English have developed a system of classes, under a hollow pretext of extra comfort and service. These extras, which are not worth anything like the cost differential, enable important people to shut themselves off from the common people for the duration of the journey. In the new "classless" England, it would be wrong to describe these different accommodations as upper class and lower class and our shipping lines and airlines have been careful to provide boats and airplanes perfectly suited to our new democracy. The expensive accommodation is described as "First Class." This would seem snobbish, would indeed *be* snobbish, if the less-expensive, more crowded accommodation were labeled "Second class." But it is not. It is "Tourist."

This convinces the lower-class traveler that, far from insulting him, the company is in fact congratulating him on his gregariousness. The actual, observable difference between one seat, or cabin, or dining room and another will be barely noticeable. What the upper-class expect for the extra money they pay is a servility differential. The sort of thing an Englishman had in mind when he wrote to the *Sunday Times*, " 'Do you gents want something to drink?' though said in a perfectly friendly manner, was not, for my view, the right way for a wine waiter to address First Class passengers."

Most travel companies achieve this servility differential by treating tourist passengers with normal politeness and first-class passengers obsequiously, though some employ the interesting variation of treating first-class passengers with ordinary politeness and insulting the others. This infuriates the first-class passengers, as it infuriated the *Sunday Times* correspondent, until they see the others being insulted, when they are mollified.

It is true, and at first sight offensive, that England's railways are unambiguously class-conscious. They are clearly marked first-class compartments and second-class compartments. This comforts the upper-class yet does not outrage the lower because our railways are old fashioned, which description, in England, absolves curious practices of many kinds. It was certainly held sufficient reason for closing down most of our branch railway lines. After all, who was going to suffer? Only the sort of people who traveled second class; people who lived in rural areas and did not own cars. Serve them right for trying to travel anyway.

Important people's transport absorbs a tremendous amount of national energy and talk and newsprint. Urban congestion (which affects businessmen's cars) BEA's behavior, BOAC's losses, passenger trains, highways, electrification of the railway lines that carry industrialists and government officers between one city and another, the building of the Q4 liner, the Concord—all these and many more aspects of our concern for and expenditure on important people's travel crop up more or less daily in the press. Even if they travel by bicycle, important people must distinguish themselves from others, as the Chief Constable of Stockport has reminded us. The Chief Constable has told members of his force that "when cycling, one should propel the pedals with the ball of the foot and not the instep. From the point of view of public appearance, I hope the practice of pedaling with the instep, and leaving the front of the foot protruding, will cease."

Everybody understands that when significant people want to travel it is right that millions of pounds of taxpayers money should be spent to ensure that they travel in style and comfort. Although the Q4 is doomed to lose money from its very first trip we all understand that it must, nevertheless, be built, justifying Bea Lillie even more in asking the question she asked on one of the Queens: "I say, what time does this place get to New York?" Equally, at the other end of the scale, everybody understands that the common people have no divine right to be traveling at all, and indeed it's time they stopped. For this reason, the bus services are being run down to almost unbelievable levels either of infrequency and unreliability or, in congested areas, in batches of five or six at once. One journalist asked a London Transport official how far their buses would stretch if placed end to end and the official told him to go out into Oxford Street and find out for himself. And the poor bus traveler's complaints carry no weight whatever, usually meriting no more than a brief mention in the newspaper correspondence columns. A bewildered Englishman wrote to the *Daily Mirror*, "I wondered why my bus was going so fast late at night. Then the conductor said: 'We're nipping along sharpish to miss the cinema crowds.'" The conductor understood perfectly well that the sort of people who use buses have no real right to be traveling at all, and that if the service gets bad enough perhaps it will teach them to stay in their place and not travel around aping their betters and trying to enjoy themselves. The London bus service offers ten times more scope for criticism and complaint than BEA, but seeing the sort of people who travel on buses, who cares?

On the whole, the English have managed fairly well

to segregate the nobles from the peasants in public transport, but there is one area of tremendous importance in which they have failed utterly. And that is the private car. What makes it particularly appalling is that, although the cars they drive make it possible to tell at a glance who are the nobles and who the peasants, both classes use exactly the same roads. So we have the terrible problem of inherent differentiation without segregation. We make it absolutely clear who is which social class, and then we all have to rub bumpers, so to speak, on the public highway. To make confusion worse, any car gives its driver delusions about himself and other people. Mr. T. F. Davies, a North London magistrate, made the point succinctly enough when he told a dustman up before him, "What with holidays in Torquay and Ford cars, you are over-reaching yourself."

Imagine an Englishman driving along in his Ford Cortina. He looks in his mirror and sees a Humber Super Snipe coming up behind him. This is not to him merely a faster, more powerful car. It is a nobleman trying to impress on him that he is a peasant. The Humber driver sounds his horn. Again, this is not to the Ford Cortina driver merely a simple communication and warning—the only one possible in the circumstances—that the Humber is about to pass. It is a nobleman using, typically, peremptory and arrogant language to a peasant. There can be only one response to such abuse. The Cortina driver veers to the crown of the road. And stays there. Smugly, he looks again in his mirror. Good God! That haughty noble is now trying to go beyond even his legal rights and cut in on the inside! The egalitarian soul, which co-exists so uncomfortably with the class-conscious mind of the Englishman, rises up inside him. The spirit that defied King John at Runnymede is not going to bow before a Humber Super Snipe, as a sudden switch to the inside lane will prove. . . .

Suppose the Ford Cortina driver survives that encounter and ten miles further on there appears before him on the crown of the road an ancient Morris Minor burbling along at 25 miles an hour. At once his role changes. *He* is now the proud nobleman whose stately progress is impeded by an idiot peasant. Did he pay £700 for his fine carriage in order to have it impeded by this broken down cart that would not fetch £25 at a charity auction? It might well be that the driver of the Morris Minor is hurrying to visit his wife in hospital; the sort of person and situation that would command all his help and sympathy in a personal situation. But in a travel situation he is merely a peasant with no right to be on the roads at all, holding up one of his betters, as demonstrated by his possession of a better car, by a mixture of incompetence and stubbornness. Meanwhile, the driver of the old Morris sees in *his* mirror that the arrogant Cortina is starting to cut inside. And *he* is not going to be treated like a peasant, as a sudden switch to the inside lane will prove. . . .

Other nationalities think the business of driving is

quite dangerous enough in itself—only the English give it extra zest by making the roads a battlefield of their class war. It accounts for something that always amazes motorists from more egalitarian countries like America and Canada—the fantastic discourtesy of the English driver towards pedestrians. They are the eternal sufferers in England's war of the roads; the people with no status at all. The driver of the most ancient and battered car can look down on the pedestrian; can feel affronted if he dares to step on to the highway which has been made for the rich and important people such as motorists. The fact that the pedestrian has probably just parked his perfectly respectable car does not save him. Once out of his car and on foot he is a peasant with ideas above his station, and he is treated as such. And ordinary pedal cyclists are not much better. One motorist wrote to the *Sun:* "During the last six months I have knocked over no fewer than four cyclists. On each occasion the cyclist was entirely to blame. In future I shall let them take the consequences of their own folly and make no effort to avoid them." In ways like this motoring in England becomes a curious new twentieth century equivalent of foxhunting, with the pedestrian the quarry.

And if the motorist is involved in an accident while his attention was diverted on to one or other of his assorted revelries, he has an answer for everything. If he hits a tree while looking the other way it is because the tree was not signposted and if he drives eighty feet over a cliff, it's all changed since he was last here. One judge once said that half the cases that came before him concerned automobile collisions in which both cars were on their own side of the road, each sounding a warning blast on its horn, and each of them stationary.

What is the solution? It must be to reproduce on the roads the class segregation we have achieved in other forms of transport. It would be quite easy, as a matter of fact, because we already have a class system on our roads. All we have to do is use it properly.

Instead of one class of private vehicle license we should have three: one of, say, £200 a year, entitling the driver to travel on A-class roads; another of perhaps £50 a year, valid for B-class roads but not A-class; and a third of £5 a year, for unclassified roads only. Highways and city center roads would be open only to people who held a pass to the Royal Enclosure at Ascot. Such a system would reduce congestion and raise large revenues. Above all, it would provide the class segregation we love so dearly—and would stop us from fighting it out on the roads every weekend with such a lethal passion.

5

The Industrial Evolution

IN virtually every other industrial country in the world, the rise of industrialism was connected with the rise of constitutional-nationalism; the pressure of the new men, many of whom had come to influence through industry, to get a say in how government was run. The consequence is that the tradition of the new ruling class in those countries, the men who overthrew or tamed the monarchies and dynasties of the preceding centuries, is sympathetically tied to industry. In such countries industry is one of the estates of the realm, a part of the establishment.

This is not the case in England. National feeling, the feeling of being English, developed in England under the Tudors, particularly Elizabeth I. This was about three hundred years earlier than in the rest of Europe, where the populations owed mere feudal allegiances to, say, a

[73]

Hapsburg, or Valois, or Bourbon prince. And when England's constitutional revolution occurred, with Cromwell, it was led by the small gentry. The result was that the new man had nothing to do with industry. The new class was broadly based in the landed people, and after fifty years of absentee monarchy by the first two Georges, these were the people in control of government. The political struggle had landowners on both sides—it was between the large landowner Whigs and the small landowner Tories. Consequently, when industry started, it was outcast from society, excluded from all the important places and discussions. It finally got a political voice in 1832, with the Reform Act, but it never got a social standing.

All through the nineteenth century and into the twentieth, industry was fairly contemptible. It was not even called industry. Most of the time it was referred to, slightingly, as "trade." Gentlemen had better things to do. There was the army, which had become glorious under Wellington; the navy, which had become glorious under Nelson; the Empire, glorified by Rhodes and Kipling; there were diplomacy and government; the Church; the learned professions; and there was the leisured life of polite society. "Trade" was so far down the list as to be out of sight to anyone of refinement and breeding. Trade was the preserve of those who sank to the squalid depths of making money. The fact that Empire-builder Cecil Rhodes made several million was excused on the grounds that money was not the object of his operations, only the by-product of his noble imperialism.

THE INDUSTRIAL EVOLUTION

Right up to the end of the second World War it remained possible to believe that Britain's greatness rested on her Commonwealth and Empire, on her army, navy and air force and the spirit of service and sacrifice. All our education, all the standards of public life and the implicit assumptions of the mass media, aspired to this ideal. It was epitomized in Eton and Sandhurst, institutionalized by Baden-Powell, popularized by Henty and Bulldog Drummond, and vulgarized by the whole Frank Wharton-Bob Cherry-Billy Bunter menagerie. The national ideal was the gentleman: aristocratic, leisured, dare-devil, chivalrous, honorable, altruistic. He could also be boneheaded, philistine, amateurish, sexless, insensitive and humorless. He could on no account be an efficient full-time manager, a thrusting salesman, an expert analyst of profit and loss accounts, or have a flair for manufacturing articles the public would buy in large numbers.

In the last twenty years, there has been the big switch. Gradually it became clear to those who control our destinies that we were in a plight from which the combined abilities of Lord Peter Wimsey and the Scarlet Pimpernel were not enough to save us. Our imperial heritage was useless; the army and the navy and the air force were no longer a shield or spearhead but a gigantic burden. We were fighting a battle for our future, but we were not fighting it with tanks and ships and planes. We were fighting it with automobiles and oil tankers and electronic equipment and high-grade steel, and all the other neglected, despised products of that unspeakable area of the demi-monde—"trade." Our future depended on *its* success, *its* international drive.

Hastily, it was given the name of industry and told to get on with the job of saving Britain, because nobody else could do it.

That was all very well in theory, but there were two slight practical difficulties. For more than a hundred years, it had been looked on as a social ghetto; a place where no one of talent or broad education or natural leadership would ever find himself if he could possibly help it. Consequently, the industrial community, by comparison with that of other nations, was something of a talent vacuum. Even now, it is staggering to think how few industrialists of real achievement are the products of an orthodox upper class public school, Oxford or Cambridge, or a well connected background.

The lack of talented leadership led to a further, perhaps more serious, fault: bad relations between employer and employee. Here, industry could certainly have learned something from the armed forces. "Labor relations" in the services does not, and did not, depend on the order-them-about-and-slap-them-on-a-charge kind of discipline that some people imagine, even though some retired officers can be heard pining for it from time to time. The essence of service discipline is that there are no bad men, only bad officers. The services insure that there is one officer to every thirty or so men, and that men are singled out for responsibility as NCO's as soon as they show that they are ready to work as leaders, on the side of the officers.

Industry was denied this training and continued in the less enlightened tradition of the mill owner and the mine owner. It let the work force choose its own leaders to *fight* management, instead of co-opting those leaders on to the side of management from the start. Rarely indeed did we hear of "a cloud of dust raised by workmen rushing to get back to work when the foreman appeared"—which was once the cause of a civil action at Westminster County Court.

But industry *did* absorb, at one remove so to speak, the more odious side of the service method, indeed the method of English society as a whole: the social segregation of the classes. And because it is always those who are the least secure socially who are the most rigid about social forms and observances and distinctions, industry created a virtual caste system, so that it became nearly impossible for a man on the shop floor to aspire to any sort of managerial responsibility. In fact, it became practically impossible for management and labor to speak to each other; there was no channel of communication between top and bottom as there is, via NCO's, in the services. The natural tension between employer and employee was increased by lack of real leadership, and then impossibly embittered by making the industrial battlefield a battlefield in the class war at the same time. Lord Saye and Sele once said in the House of Lords, "The hereditary system is the only method of selecting a body of people which is completely unbiased. Every other method, except perhaps lottery, must depend on somebody's opinion." Industry leaned heavily on his lordship's principles (not that this gave it access to the House of Lords). For many years, "labor relations" in England meant a man was the lucky son of the founder of the company. And every Christmas, at the works party, he did his best to prove he was just an ordinary, friendly working man. Clutching a mug full of warm beer, he would embrace riveter Jackson like a long-lost son with the cheering words "Merry Christmas, Jenkins!"

Still, now that industry has been told how vital it is to our prosperity, it has begun to put some of these matters right. It is the problems outside industry which are really troublesome. The economic climate may change in a few years, but social taboos and ingrained class assumptions last a lifetime. And we have to face the fact that none of the topmost of the upper class, the people in the most respected positions in the land, are interested in industry; most of them, in fact, despise it. They may pretend that they think industry is splendid, especially if it can get us out of debt so that we can decide our own foreign and economic policies instead of having them dictated to us by the United States and Zurich, but in their hearts they still thank God that they have nothing to do with it.

Civil Service people sneer at it, telling each other over coffee every morning how they could have made a packet in it with their brains if they had not preferred doing something useful for their country instead of simply filling their own pockets. They make little effort to support it, buying equipment from America quite happily, even when they could do virtually as well with the product of their own industry. They totally mistrust industrialists and assume that they are always being cheated—assuming further that industry makes a practice of charging the nation three men's pay for two men's work done in one man's time. Instead of trying, as many governments do, to cut themselves in on the profits of successful enterprises, they stay aloof and disapproving. Every now and then an investigation turns up evidence of industry's overcharging the government (as the Ferranti company did), which convinces them of the contrast between the murky morals of industry and their own lily-whiteness.

The universities, at least the older ones, also find industry despicable. They cannot say so out loud because so much of their research is financed by it, but both they and their brightest undergraduates regard it as the direst failure if they have to have something positive and direct to do with it.

Parliament dislikes it because it represents power beyond their control, indeed beyond their comprehension, since very few members understand what really makes it tick. To the Church it represents, quite simply, Mammon, though of course any old bishop will turn out to bless a new factory if called upon to do so, in the pious hope of acquiring a few converts. To the armed forces it is still a hideout for people who are neither gentlemen nor know the meaning of service. The service mind can still only follow and accept the simplest concepts. The popular press does not understand it at all. Its heroes are still models and sportsmen and politicians and photographers. It goes on at amazing length about all sorts of people of no power or significance or interest, leaving its readers in total ignorance of the men on whom it is said their future depends, unless it is something which it is impossible even for them to ignore, like ICI bidding for the Monopolies Commission. If television touches industry it is only to turn it into high-life personality dramas. It spends interminable time on political un-news, but hardly ever gives industry a look-in except as a factor in politics. Most of the semi-serious mass-media organs are steeped in the *Observer* magazine section liberal-aesthetic attitude toward life, and to them industry is something in which greedy men exploit poor workers to line their own pockets; something in which there is no art and no politics and is therefore to be classified as Not Interesting.

But it is, above all, the scorn of society which is so oppressive to industry. At the very top of the pyramid, the Royals do their duty manfully, going around the world in the interest of exports and, more conspicuously, going around Britain to raise the flagging spirits of the workers. One or two top industrialists are vaguely noble, but the great mass of successful industrialists, many of them self-made men who "came up the hard way" are regarded, socially, as crumbs. The highest rank they may aspire to is only "captain of industry." Any charity hostess would think herself very hard up if she was reduced to the chairman of onc of our big industrial combines as guest of honor at her party. Everyone would know she had been turned down by half the peers in Debrett followed by half the actors in *Spotlight*. Industry depends on engineers—mechanical, electrical, civil, electronic, chemical and so on—and in many countries they are the social elite. But the very words, in England, suggest someone who has just taken off his oily overalls. Even Public Relations Officer rates higher socially.

The result, apart from being insulting and infuriating to a lot of industrialists, is disastrous. In most other countries, there is a top network who meet both professionally and socially; who are involved with one another's worlds and have a fair understanding of one another's jobs. It includes the government, the top civil servants, the press, the bankers, the industrialists and the universities. This is so in the United States and most of Europe. In England, the industrialists are either left out altogether or else treated as if they were of no great importance. This results in a very poor flow of the sort of information and informal discussion that is so extremely valuable to industrialists, giving them a hint of what is in the air diplomatically or financially, giving them lines of contact to express their opinion or to seek or offer advice. Even when our industrialists are being briefly courted for an export drive, they are infelicitously told that it is "their duty to the country" or that they should "play the game," whereas anyone who knows even the slightest bit about industry knows that the only incentive is a good return on shareholders' investment, either now or in the forseeable future.

But *that* idea, of course, is not at all in the spirit of Dunkirk or Greyfriars.

6

Sin

AT THE root of the English way of life lies the Englishman's attitudes toward sin. The origins of these attitudes
are buried deep in history but they erupted in the seven-
teenth century, when the common man's party, the left
wing Roundheads, became identified with an austere, puritan morality; while the right wing Royalists and Cavaliers
showed a preference for a more indulgent and voluptuous
existence. From these roots there have grown two separate
views of sin. They show themselves most vividly when they
are applied to money.

The upper class right wing says: "Everyone should
have money, but if they haven't got it, it is sinful to try to
get it." It will be obvious, therefore, that the right wing
are implacably opposed, on what they claim are *moral*
grounds, to strikes, working mothers, national assistance,
betting and any other situations in which, plainly, people
are trying to get hold of extra, undeserved money. Their
sin consists in "letting the country down when it's in a
tight corner," which it always is.

Members of the young generation of the 1960's attract particular condemnation because they so blatantly prove what the right wing have always suspected: that all the money the right wing have nobly disgorged for maternity benefits, welfare food, national health, family allowances, education, unemployment benefit and national assistance was not merely received without gratitude, but was so unnecessary that it has all been spent on motor scooters, outrageous clothing, guitars, and cups of espresso coffee; and not a penny on haircuts. The younger generation is regarded by the right wing as slothful, lustful and avaricious. They are not a patch on their parents, will never amount to anything, don't know the difference between right and wrong, and won't listen. In short, the last sin for which the rich will never forgive the poor is a display of wealth. And the first virtue they will applaud is a determination to stay poor.

One member of the younger generation who was chairwoman of a youth club scandalized the club patrons, the vicar, and the local squire when she performed at a fund-raising show an act which, though described as a strip-tease, was nevertheless so modest as to be indistinguishable from a school gymnastic display. They asked her to resign. She said she had meant no harm. They insisted she resign. A little later, they heard she had refused an offer of £100 to repeat her act in a London club. Turning away money like that really proved to them that she was not sinful. They re-appointed her to her office.

Quite horrifying to the right wing is the idea that

wives should work and try to bring family incomes of those who haven't money somewhere nearer the level of those who have. Unpaid social work is acceptable to them, and so is doing a job "for the fun and interest" of it. But for a wife to work straightforwardly for money is reprehensible, because the right wing believe that, by means of their personal charity known as the Welfare State, they have already provided the poor with everything they need apart from bread. But, of course, to protest against people trying to get themselves a little extra comfort or luxury would be too starkly resentful, so the protest is always angled toward the harm it does to the children, the poor "latchkey kids" who have to do without their mothers for an hour or so a day. Meanwhile, the right wing happily send their own children off to boarding schools, where they have to do without their mothers for eight months a year. That, however, is quite different, since it costs them money instead of giving them the opportunity to earn it.

The right wing concept of liberty is theoretically broad enough to include the freedom to take a week off from work in the coal mine or in the shipyard any time a man feels it is getting him down. But to the right wing—reading about it during their winter holiday in St. Moritz—this is absenteeism; a flagrant sin implying that the lazy fellow does not need the money for that week's work, so why did they ever bother to pay out for the ante-natal clinic, the state education, national assistance etc. etc.

Living on national assistance is, itself, an unspeakable

sin. The right wing regard it as a frightful swindle on themselves and sheer theft of their money. Yet, oddly, they regard with ill-concealed amusement something like the Ferranti £4½ million coup at the nation's expense and are perfectly satisfied that the bondwashers who found a way of doing the Exchequer out of £37 million should keep it. The train robbers, on the other hand, caught the full fury of the law and the undiluted indignation of the right wing because they were poor people, behaving the way some poor people behave, yet getting the sort of loot—£2½ million—that is only tolerable if it is acquired by a Stock Exchange coup. The misfortune of the train robbers was that they tried to sin on a level that was out of their class.

The lower class left wing sees things in an altogether different way from the right wing upper class. They say "nobody should have money, but, if they have, it is sinful to enjoy it." So they are implacably opposed on what they claim are moral grounds to profits, dividends, inherited wealth, large houses, creature comforts, and luxuries.

The fact that it is the hope of profit which has been the drive behind just about every improvement in man's material welfare is ignored by the left, on whom the mere word "profit" has the same shocking effect as the word "orgy." But it is above all the enjoyment of money that horrifies the left wing. Their chagrin was expressed most acutely when it became known that Mr. Nigel Lawson, the editor of a right wing periodical, had borrowed £30,000 of public money in order to buy a house for himself and his family. The money came from funds properly set aside to help intending house purchasers; Mr. Lawson's application and the acceptance of it were both perfectly above board; no other house-hunter suffered because of his piece of business; the terms of the loan were onerous. Yet there issued from the left a most appalling screech of dismay. One might have imagined that Mr. Lawson had stolen the money after bashing the cashier, so noisily was he besought to give it back. The economics and the politics of the matter were bandied about with great spirit, though little sense. But behind all the ridiculous noise and confusion there was a very genuine left wing feeling—a feeling of both terror and disgust that anyone should be so wicked as to pay so much for a house at all.

The hatred of Jaguars is only an instance of the left wing feeling that it is in fact sinful to own a Jaguar. The Labor Government's 70 m.p.h. limit has only met hostility because Morris Minors and Anglias can top 70. A limit of 90, perhaps even 80, would have been universally welcomed, but the impulse to put an upper speed limit at all was an aspect of the idea that fast driving is somehow sinful in itself.

Comfort and ease of any kind are anathema to the left. Their view of sin is epitomized in their attitude toward a thick carpet. A thick carpet makes a left-winger very uneasy. He does not like it at all. At first sight, like so many dangerous objects, it seems utterly innocent and friendly. But a thick carpet is not harmless. On the contrary. First, it is expensive. That is bad. Second, it could make you feel cozy. That is worse. Thirdly, it could lead to impromptu love-making. Which is unthinkable. So temptation and sin are avoided by the purchase of an honest piece of linoleum. Similarly virtuous are open windows, angular chairs, narrow beds, plain food, abrasive towels, and carbolic soap.

Again, it is unforgivable to sin out of your class. The poor woman who won a fortune on the football pools and then said, quite naturally but so rashly, that she was going to "spend, spend, spend" was roundly vilified by the left. The virtuous thing to say would have been that it would make no difference to her life at all, that she would keep at her job, and go on living in the same way in the same street where all her real friends were. Later her story of her spending spree was dressed up in the press as a "confession."

The result of these two English attitudes toward sin is an extraordinary amalgam of laws and prejudices. But there is a clear thread running through them. The sins of the left must be uncomfortable, and the sins of the right must be expensive. Neither side wants actually to *stop* sinning. All that the English require of their wrongdoing is that the right shall make sure the left suffer for it, and that the left shall make sure the right pay for it. For the Englishman is in favor of sin, but opposed to the open enjoyment of it. He wants lots of opportunity to sin, but he wants also to be sure that even as he sins he is suffering either physical discomfort or financial loss. He wants the pleasures of sin and atonement. And he wants them both at the same time. In short, he likes to commit adultery in a hair shirt, absolved by a sort of moral Pay-As-You-Earn.

Parliament went to a great deal of trouble a few years ago to regulate the sin of gambling. It could have been made completely illegal, or completely irreproachable. But neither would have accorded with an Englishman's sense of right and wrong. The law was elaborately framed so that the right could gamble in luxurious and very expensive high-stake casinos and clubs and the left could gamble in betting shops—which are by statute prohibited even from having chairs to sit on. Thus, the left wing made sure the right paid heavily for their sinning, and the right made sure the left were thoroughly uncomfortable for theirs. Even on something as tame as the pools, the English like to be addressed not as "gamblers" but "investors," hoping not for "winnings" but "dividends."

The *Evening Standard's* late political cartoonist Vicky expressed the moral contortions into which the English attitude toward sin forces people when he depicted Mr. R. A. Butler saying, in a mood of self-congratulation: ".There, we've done it. We've got the prostitutes off the street, and we have brought gambling out into the open."

Drink is ruled by the same consideration as gambling. The rich can drink their wines and liquor at home at any hour of the day, or in restaurants, or the hotel they are staying in, or on their planes and boats. But these are expensive drinks and expensive places, and, since liquor is much more expensive than beer, they are taxed much more heavily because they are what the right chooses to get drunk on. The poor, on the other hand, drink their beer under the auspices of a set of licensing laws that make it as difficult as possible to get into the pub for a drink whenever they feel like it, and as easy as possible for them to be turfed out just when they are starting to enjoy themselves.

Naturally, there are some evils against which right and lefts unite. The English are all agreed that a group of girls who went for a naked moonlight swim in a lake in Warwickshire were utterly reprehensible and it was quite right to establish a police patrol to see that it did not happen again. For, as the police said, the girls were a source of embarrassment and annoyance to courting couples who lurk beneath bushes around the lake.

They are united, too, in their willingness to hear confessions of really serious sin. They have done away with the parish priest in this function, and, appropriately enough, the Sunday newspapers have replaced the confessional box. Read "How I Held Strange Black Magic Rites in a Luxury Trailer. How I Sailed the Atlantic with Five Beautiful Girls in a One-Berth Sloop. How I Attended Wife-Swapping Parties with an Attractive 32-year-old Brunette. How I Opened a Boys' Club Despite My Previous Criminal Record. Let *MY* Dreadful Shame Be a Warning to *YOU*. Read My Confessions Today." Such sinners are granted immediate absolution and, far from being forced into sackcloth and ashes, they are given big fat checks into the bargain.

And both left and right understand perfectly the ambiguous language with which, nowadays, the English literary critics cloak descriptions of sin. Thus, they appreciate that "Rabelaisian" means "filthy." "A sensitive and tender story of young love"—"Filthy." "A vivid social document"—"Really filthy." "A book I finally warmed to" —"The filthy bits are at the end." "A book I could not finish"—"The filthy bits are at the beginning." "An erotic masterpiece"—Nineteenth century sadism. "An erotic classic"—Pre-nineteenth century sadism.

But whereas the English prefer not to buy a book which is described straightforwardly as wicked, they prefer to go to films that are. So we get "They were two primitive beasts, clawing each other with naked passion" to describe *Born Free*. "A side of London's teenage vice that will shock you" for *Oliver Twist*. And "trapped in the bed of a beast" for *Goldilocks*. What you will rarely find is the totally innocent film, totally innocently described: "We bring to the screen the other side of Soho, a strange world, the world of decency. Scenes never before shown—including an Italian fully dressed, opening a can of sardines, a young girl fresh from the provinces writing home to her mother and asking her to send a cake, and two schoolmasters spending the evening together doing the *Daily Telegraph* crossword."

On the whole though, apart from the fundamental

sins connected with money and class, there is little that the English consider downright immoral. There is, of course, the occasional eccentric, like the woman giving evidence at Ilford County Court who said she objected to seeing men's pajamas hanging on a clothes line "in an indiscreet way." Or the man, mentioned in the annual report of the Law Society, who told his lawyer to start proceedings for divorce, then a few days later told him to stop "in case my wife gets to hear about it." Such people— and the headmistress of a senior girls' school who beseeches her pupils not to wear patent leather shoes "else men will see your underwear reflected in them"—are the exception rather than the rule. Most of the English rather like sin, so long as they only see it sidelong.

In general, they take their lead from the Reverend Cyril Downes. When Mr. Downes, a Methodist minister, heard that some Sheffield students were putting on a production of Oscar Wilde's *Salome,* he went over and had a heart-to-heart talk with them. The result was that when the leading lady, in the words of the *Daily Mail* "peeled off the last of her seven veils, she stood revealed in a flared skirt and tunic blouse. With sleeves." As de Madariaga said: "The Anglo-Saxon conscience does not prevent the Anglo-Saxon from sinning. It merely prevents him from enjoying it."

7

Sex

LOVE makes the world go round; marriage makes it go flat. It seemed an exceptionally cynical remark when first made by George Bernard Shaw at the beginning of the century. But consider this advertisement in the *Evening Standard*: "Wanted—Playpen, cot and high chair. Also two single beds."

In just ten words, some young English couple tell us they feel they have crossed the thin line that separates love from hate, called marriage, and are ready for the dead, flat world beyond. Out of the world of the pop song, which presents sex without love, into the world of the television commercial, which presents love without sex.

Where have all the young men gone? In the world of the television commercial, it seems that they have gone to hubbies, every one. In the world of the television commercial, which has taken us far along the road to an American-type matriarchy, all passion was spent long, long ago and the young men have become old and querulous before their time. They prepare for their strongest feelings by having a feather-touch shave, attending to their personal freshness, eating a meal rich with man-appeal and drinking a gallon of milk. Thus girded up and heavy with sexual promise, they actually consummate their feelings with a box of after-dinner mint chocolates. Not that one can altogether blame them, for where have all the young girls gone? Gone to housewives, every one, busy each witching hour preparing sleep-inducing drinks to pour down the throats of the men they are married to; anything to keep them quiet while they get on with adding an egg to the wonder cake mix.

So where did all the kids come from? Well, just as the world of telly ads convinces us that post-marital intercourse is non-existent, so the world of pop songs convinces us that pre-marital intercourse is universal. Perhaps that's where the kids come from. In olden days, a man rescued a damsel in distress and married her. These days, he still rescues a damsel in distress and marries her. These days, however, he's probably the one who got her in distress in the first place.

Ever since the cave man first began to grunt, the archetypal love song has been warm, romantic, idyllic, chivalrous; he has sighed and pined for his beloved, sometimes hymning her praises, sometimes pining her departure. Underlying his song has always been the assumption that his love is true and enduring and that his idea of paradise is to be with her forever. Suddenly this has changed. An element has been subtracted. And it was the vital element. The new archetype is a love song without love. It is not about a lifetime in heaven, it's about a night in bed. The Rolling Stones' hit number, "This Could Be The Last Time," is a typical example. It is not the anguished lover saying he'll kill himself if his beloved doesn't say she loves him; it is the self-centered young man telling his bird that if she doesn't sleep with him tonight she need not expect him to take her out again. It is difficult to lament the passing of the old love songs, with their spurious emotions, but the new have gone to the other extreme in reducing everything to the lowest glandular denominator. The young English have overtaken the French, who regard love as a pleasant diversion between meals, and are fast catching up with the Swedes, who regard it as a pleasant diversion during meals.

But, once again, how can one blame the youngsters and their pop idols? Convinced by television that marriage is a terrible monasticism in which all fathers can do is give presents, romp occasionally with the happy, milk-fed children, get rid of his lumbago with New Formula, and watch his personal freshness. In this same monastic marriage, the preparation and consumption of proprietary brands of food is a substitute for making love—and the youngsters, not surprisingly, conclude that they had better have one hell of an orgy while they still have time. In doing so, they produce the statistics that show that people are getting married younger and having their first babies sooner, but not necessarily in that order.

One young man was a witness against another in a

recent case of assault. The defendant was accused of walking up to a girl outside a dance hall and trying to rip her dress off. The girl was the witness's fiancee. He was with her at the time.

"What did you do when this happened?" he was asked.

"Well, nothing."

"Nothing! Do you mean to tell the court you just stood there while this brute came up to your girl and tried to tear her dress off her back?"

"Well," he said, "I thought he might be someone she knew."

And so, indeed, he might have been, for case after case in our courts indicates how fast and freely people get around nowadays.

Yet while the young seem to exult in their new-found relationships, there is another older, more romantically disappointed generation. How English is this divorce case reported by the *Evening News*: "The wife told the judge that, after confessing to her husband about her adultery with an itinerant ice cream seller, she wrote a letter to the ice cream man ending the association. She gave it to her husband, who took it to the man, shook hands with him, and came back with two sixpenny cones."

An ice cream cone is a mild insult to a woman compared with that offered by another husband. His wife claimed that she first realized love had died when he started to miss with the things he threw at her. This was part of the evidence in her divorce petition, but the judge thought much more telling the fact that the husband had recently abandoned a habit she had always appreciated as a little token of tenderness—looking at their wedding photographs as they lay making love. "Sometimes he does this one, sometimes he does the other, but never both together now, that's what upsets me so," she told the sympathetic court.

The English husband learns quickly enough once he has married that sexuality is a weapon used more skillfully, in the long run, by an English woman than an English man. Unable, or unwilling, to pay the high price—understanding and tenderness—she now demands for new favors, he settles back into the mood of "Take my wife—please" caught so accurately by generations of vaudeville comics.

It is not therefore surprising that the new rampant youth finds itself being received rather like G.I.'s during the war: they're over-paid, over-sexed, and over here. But unlike the American soldiers, they're here to stay: which makes them more of a problem.

It is as if a vast army of aliens had come amongst us, wearing different clothes and different hair, observing different customs and worshipping different idols; this great mass of "young people" so different from ourselves, and so alluring, that one might as easily be saying "Japanese" or "Martians." Gradually and painfully, we assimilate them into our society, but there are always more of them arriving and the problem, far from being solved, becomes more and more acute. England's youth are all living with each other; they ignore or insult their parents and teachers; they break into houses and beat up old ladies; they have no respect, no discipline, no morals. They are out taking drugs while their parents are safely tucked up in bed with eight whiskies and two sleeping pills inside them; they have sex orgies when respectable people are reading the *News of the World;* they waste their lives listening to pop groups while their parents are seeing "The Sound of Music" for the 133rd time.

They think only of themselves and their clothes; they are all like the girl at Chester Assizes who, asked by the judge why she took off her slip in her boy's friend's car on a Saturday night, said: "It was rather an expensive one and I knew what we were going to do. I asked him if I could take it off as I did not want to get it crumpled." According to *The Observer,* all this can be ascribed to "Artificial development. Outsize vegetables grown with 'boosters,' cows which produce far more milk than they were designed by nature to do, hens which never see daylight—and now our overdeveloped children, stuffed with vitamins from birth. With our unsuitable climate, they were never intended to reach sexual maturity until at least fifteen."

They not only have money to burn; now they are trying to smoke it as well. We all feel slightly superior to young people, as we did to G.I.'s, but we have to worship them and court their favor in order to get a portion of their big pay packets. We have to learn phrases like "dig" and "gritty" just as we once had to learn phrases like "swell" and "you're welcome," in the hope of a hand-out from the wad of notes in G.I. wallets. Whereas, in the old days, we had to save up all our lives to have a little money to spend in our old age, these bounders have the money while they are still young enough to enjoy it: for the first time in England's history it sometimes seems that the average pocket money is more than the average old-age pension. Youth has so much, in fact, that it is reported that the Plymouth City Council, for example, "took away its £100 grants from two homes for unmarried mothers and teen-age girls and gave them instead to Plymouth Dogs and Cats Homes." Or to quote the words of one middle-aged man: "The main thing I've got against this new morality is that it wasn't going when I was young."

The whole pattern of the middle-aged, middle-browed core of the nation has been inverted in the last few years. Today's middle-aged grew up in a culture in which you began as a poor student or apprentice, started to earn a bit more after you got married, and finally entered into your inheritance when you were in your fifties and the children were off your hands. The last years were the affluent ones. These people, now in their late forties or over, grew up in the slump years, worked and slaved and denied themselves pleasures in order to have something left at the end. Now, they see young people doing it all the other way round, for which they both adore and revile them. They feel a bit like Tallulah Bankhead, who visited a family with a particularly spoiled and obnoxious teen-aged son. "We just don't know what to make of him," said his mother. "How about a nice rug?" suggested Miss Bankhead.

In this decade, the English have the richest time of their lives in their teens. They are well-paid, independent, unencumbered. But they know that the next stage will not be so good; slightly better paid, perhaps, but with a family to take care of; discretionary spending power will be much less; and the final stage on the old age pension will be worse still. So they enjoy the fruits of their old age now, with only the deprivations of youth to look forward to. In short, the means for enjoyment are available at the peak of sexual vigor and physical fitness and mental alertness, instead of way past it. There was a time when English teenage girls lived with their parents. Now, they all want to move into bachelor apartments. Most of them don't wait until the bachelors have moved out. And once the boys and girls are together, they can take up the idea mooted in "Taste of Honey:" "Instead of the usual going-steady 'his' and 'hers' sweaters, my boy-friend and I are having identical color rinses for our hair, with matching high-lights. This does not cost nearly as much as sweaters, and also has the advantage that, if you break up, you can wash it out to show other boys you are in the running again." One way or another, the only pre-marital experience they seem to deny themselves is cooking.

In the days when every other Englishman could write

a love sonnet, our women were bathed in a constant tide of flattery and adoration; now, they have to be thankful for the smallest second-hand mercy. A novelty card saying "Hi, there, fatface! Happy trip to the launderette," on wedding anniversaries, for example. Joke cards and pop songs, these are the blunt instruments of an Englishman's courtship. And of the two, the cards are the more evocative and tender, for it is perfectly plain that the love songs are concerned strictly with sex. The word "love" is still used, but the sentiment and the rest of the words make more sense if the word "sex" is put in its place: This is a sexy way to spend an evening. You made me have sex with you, I didn't want to do it. Sex walked right in. You brought a new kind of sex to me. Sex is a many-splendored thing. Seduce me or leave me. Once I had a secret sex. These are the yelps of the young English wolf, the rogue male. His long hair is not a mark of femininity; it is the mark of the free-roaming animal, arrogant, assertive, sexual. Just as he has adapted love songs, so he adapts our well-meaning old proverbs for his own insolent purposes. See a woman, pick her up, all the day you'll have good luck. A woman saved is a woman earned. Procrastination is the thief of a good time. Familiarity breeds children.

It is, in fact, the combination of "artificial development" and affluence among our youth that has had such a galvanic effect upon the older generation of Englishmen. Brought up to extreme sexual restraint before a late marriage—often after it, as well—they see no sign of restraint in the next generation; brought up to save their money, they see youth spending. They are, understandably, resentful and jealous. They entered into their own inheritance too late to enjoy it and they are righteously angry when they see all these young people having a whale of a time now. No wonder that "during one month various adults have insulted my girl-friend and I and chased us from three shop doorways, three front gardens and four drafty alleyways," as one of the youngsters complained in *Weekend* magazine. All the world loves a lover, but policemen still carry flashlights.

In such a situation, logic does not stand a chance. There is no objective evidence that young people are any better or worse than their parents. They seem to have a more or less average share of the weak and the wicked and the lecherous. But evidence only very rarely comes into this debate; for the simple reason that the resentment is not one of mind, but of matter, a resentment heightened by the fact that the older generations not only see the young behaving in their badly brought up manner, but realize they have paid all the bills for the bringing-up. Unfortunately, it does not seem to have been much help, though there are reasons for this.

There is something that we call education. It happens whenever the older help the younger to develop their skills, to realize their innate abilities, to discover new interests and wider horizons, to stretch themselves beyond what they previously thought to be their limit, to formulate their areas of ignorance into precise questioning, and to pursue those questions until they receive answers which satisfy them. It happens whenever the older pass on and explain to the younger the skill, techniques, discoveries, ideas, and creative works of earlier generations; whenever they help them to come to a proper understanding of themselves, their emotional drives and irrational desires and intellectual processes, and to acquire an imaginative insight into the emotions and beliefs and desires and fears which rule their fellow men. It happens between parent and child, teacher and pupil, craftsman and apprentice. It is the force which has created the civilized world.

This kind of education, however, is not what anyone is referring to when they talk about Education. It is, after all, extremely demanding, and cannot possibly be carried on day after day by a single teacher with 40 pupils. And yet 40 pupils is the acceptable norm in British primary schools; there are many classes of over 50. We may therefore take it that Education has nothing to do with education. If some real education does happen in the process of it, it must be a mixture of good luck and extraordinarily high qualities in the teacher; it cannot have been in the minds of those who ordained that Education should take place.

Examinations are a tremendous obstacle to education's taking place. They force every child to be one kind of child, and they force the school to create a system which subordinates real education to an artificial exercise called "passing exams." Children are as different as flowers in a garden. Some flowers are tall, some broad, some bright-colored, some fragrant, some hardy, some luxuriant; some children are quick-minded, some clever with their hands, some creative, some good at games, some natural leaders; all are also a combination of some of the other qualities. Real education helps each child to develop and use his own qualities as fully as possible, just as good horticulture treats each plant with lime or peat or bone meal, much or little water, sun or shade, thinning or pruning, to help it to its best state.

The skills of education and horticulture lie in differing treatments. But exams are about similarity, arbitrarily picking one or two characteristics and attaching all the importance to them, so that (educationally) carnations may go through their whole lives with a stigma of inferiority because they weren't hollyhocks. Try going through all the newspaper files for an outburst against the standard of teaching in any primary or secondary school. Try even finding criticism of one teacher on the grounds of the quality of his teaching. Not one. But can all the third of a million teachers be so good? Of course not: but no one has any way of measuring, or certainly not any way of convincing others (magistrates, juries) that their standard of measurement is valid. Now go through the newspapers again, looking this time for criticisms of the state of school buildings. That's another matter. Plenty of that. Well, you can photograph a "slum school," anyone can identify it. And councils are full of builders willing to tell the press, for pressure to rebuild and perhaps the contract for their firm. So the money is spent on bricks and mortar instead of gowns and mortar boards, and we reaffirm our preference for having children badly educated in good buildings, rather than well-educated in old buildings.

Since we have given up all hope of measuring the majority of the education that happens by quality, we measure it by quantity instead, like a prison sentence. The only concern is with how much of it children have, how long they serve. There is an elaborate system of school attendance officers to make sure children go to school, but no system to discover if they have derived any benefit from being there. Educational improvement means raising the leaving age by a year; no one ever suggests that education could be reformed by using the existing years a lot better. While it is palpably ludicrous to measure education purely by bulk, it is what we all in fact do. Ever heard of a child's being kept on at school beyond leaving age because his education hadn't been good enough?

Because nobody knows what education actually achieves, it comes readily to hand as a panacea. Its original purpose is totally forgotten or ignored, and it is held up as a last bastion against youth, as a means of stopping crime and hooliganism, of cutting down illegitimacy and reducing birth rates, and of making Britain more competitive industrially. It is the breadth of the word that causes confusion: you end up arguing that because we need more mathematics and physics graduates, we must keep secondary pupils at school for another year and do more television programs about the instruments of the orchestra. "More education" is a marvelous political battle cry because everybody believes it is true and no one can prove you wrong anyway. "Better education" only seems to imply that you're attacking those wonderful, underpaid teachers.

Clearly the answer to the whole youth problem is to raise the school-leaving age to 48. That will satisfy everybody. It will keep the bounders out of mischief, please the politicians, and fit in with the current system because it is becoming clear anyway that whoever education may be for at the moment it is certainly not for children.

8

Women

IT WAS, of course, the women of England, led by Mrs. Pankhurst, who fought the pioneer battles that have resulted, not only in England but in America and Europe too, in equality with men. It was in this century and in this country that the age of the free woman was born and nourished. A hundred years ago, women had no vote, few property rights, and could not enter politics or the professions. At the same time, a man could—and many did—quite legally support his mistress on his wife's earnings, or on the income from her property, or by the sale of her jewels.

Today, after a bitter and stubborn fight, an Englishwoman is every bit as good as an Englishman. She is his equal. An enlightened civilization has freed her from the menial tasks and irrational taboos that circumscribed her grandmother, and she is free to enter hand-in-hand with man into the promised land, sharing as a full partner in the abundant harvest of modern life. The English can be proud of this remarkable achievement; the men no less than the women, for the men renounced, with reasonable grace, much that was important to them in order that their womenfolk should be able to take their proper place in society. Which is at the kitchen sink.

For where are the women of England today? Of course they can become judges, and one of them has. Of course they can become doctors, and seven or eight have reached the top of their profession. Certainly they can become politicians, and about one in twenty-five members of Parliament is a woman. Assuredly they can have equal pay—in such jobs as teaching and nursing, where the low rates of pay are in any case a public scandal. The few Englishwomen who achieve eminence are merely a tiny token force, who serve to conceal from the rest that their position is not really much changed from the nineteenth century. Ninety-five per cent of Englishwomen are still, essentially, domestic servants, waiting on men and doing men's bidding. Secretaries? With their forethought, tact, charm and constant ministering to the wants and whims of the boss, they are performing half of the functions of a wife; three-quarters, if he is lucky. Shop assistants? The old-fashioned serving wenches, given a new label to conceal the old subservience. Factory workers? For the most part, they have been recruited for, and assigned to, the jobs that require finicky but simple neatness and dexterity, similar to their old skills of weaving, sewing, knitting and embroidery; and now they are supervised and controlled by men in a much more rigorous manner than their down-trodden mothers ever were.

Even such pathetic tottering steps as women have taken towards actual emancipation are, it is clear, deeply resented and feared and laughed at by men, who like to try and portray them as impractical, and incapable of holding a coherent conversation.

"Well, I know for a fact their place is always like a pig sty because I saw him going off to work with his umbrella up only last Tuesday—I tell a lie—Wednesday, and I thought to myself at the time why does he wear those funny ties, yes you do remember him she's got a long nose, well Rose turned round and said 'He never takes me anywhere' so if that's the best she can do I said it's no wonder they all come in for their tea at any old hour of the day and night. Well, then he turned round and gave me this look just like Rock Hudson that made me feel all peculiar. Anyway, her story is she didn't get a wink of sleep all night. . . . I must go and have a sit down I've been on my feet all day. Bye bye. . . . Hallo Jane. I was just ringing up to. . . . Oh, it's you, Tom. . . . Hallo Audrey. I just rang up Jane and I know for a fact their phone's in the bedroom. Of course I always said she'd taken on a handful there. Can't stand men who wear woolly socks. I didn't wash that blanket after all, the man called about the leak so I'll have to run down to the shops before they shut. A *white* wedding. Oh, she wouldn't *dare*. . . ."

Every Englishman believes, although every Englishman would deny it, that the vast majority of women are, or should be, serfs. Which is not to say slaves. The English are opposed to slavery, but not to serfdom. The serfs of olden days had all sorts of legal rights and even one or two privileges; but they were not allowed to leave the land. They were tied to the soil. And men believe that women should be tied, in the same way, to the soil. Unfortunately for Mrs. Pankhurst, most Englishwomen agree with them. The feminist in England has no fiercer adversary than women.

Any couple who really believe in equality, and practice it, encounter scorn and hostility. If they decide not to have children—a matter, clearly, for them alone and, in an already over-populated country, a socially reasonable decision—they will be told they don't know what they're missing (waiting seven minutes at the bottom of an escalator for a dropped lollipop to come around again, for instance), that children cement marriage and that a childless wife is not a real woman. They will be told all sorts of things to cover up the truth, which is that Englishwomen, still comforting themselves with a far-fetched piece of nonsense uttered by an Englishman at the end of the last century to put them in their place (and used by Englishmen ever since to keep them in it): "The hand that rocks the cradle is the hand that rules the world," are afraid that if they do not have a baby they will not have a husband. They know their men want them to stay at home and not go wandering about in the great big world making sensible remarks and intelligent observations; the only plausible reason for staying at home is because there is a baby in it; and in any case, children need a mother; therefore have children. And any woman who doesn't is thought to be committing an outrage against both nature and common sense.

Equally severe is the hostility toward women who have children and jobs as well. If the family is poor and really needs the money, then her action is more or less condoned, though, of course, the children are thought of as "poor little mites." But if the husband has a good, well-paid job, then the working mother is wicked. In fact, lazy! Avoiding her responsibilities! Because children need a mother. In fact, children need a father, too, but he is not wicked, lazy and irresponsible because he goes out to work, or because he spends Saturday and Sunday playing golf. It is obvious that concern for the welfare of the children is not the real reason for disapproval. It is that Englishmen and English-women are actually afraid of a woman who enjoys any sort of freedom.

This is particularly vivid in their attitude toward women drivers. Driving a car is a special kind of freedom, and to see a woman doing it stirs up the deepest wells of anger, resentment, and fear in Englishmen and their serf-women. Their contempt for women drivers in general is in fact an expression of their fear of any particular woman who shows that there is nothing in their nature to prevent all women from behaving—in all things—rationally and competently, *if they want to*. And so they develop the myth that there is something suspect about a good woman driver.

Like the childless wife, she is not a real woman; she is trying to ape her male superiors. No real woman would want to do that. Englishmen and serf-women accept the existence of women drivers only if they openly acknowledge their inferiority in this ludicrously simple activity. Thus a woman is free to drive without serious reproach *so long as she drives badly*. So long as she is skittish and careless and "feminine" and conforms to the jokes, and says, "Let's park here and walk to the curb," and so on.

Of course, given the right woman with the right man, a woman will in the last resort to do what her man wants anyway. It is the hopelessly unambitious nature of what an Englishman wants from—and for—his women that is so disturbing. The wife who had to spend her day indoors, and has nothing to report, is preferred to the wife who had been out and really achieved some acclaim in her own right. And the amazing thing is the way the women of England acquiesce in this arrangement. Deaf to appeals to break even the most unnecessary of their bonds, they join in the conspiracy, worked out by men anxious to preserve their simple right to three square meals a day and a cozy bed at night, that they are by nature fragile, impractical, and irrational. They subscribe in their millions to women's magazines—owned and run by men—which propagate the idea that a woman is completely fulfilled if she can master a moderately complicated knitting pattern, cook a small roast of beef, keep her sink tidy and teach her children not to take candy from strangers.

WOMEN

Television advertising, a part of the communications industry even more finely calculated, and even more potent, than magazine publishing and again entirely directed by men, characterizes a woman as a creature dominated by a naive belief in magic. If she is not married, her days are overwhelmed by the search for garments which will endow her bosom, loins and legs with supernatural powers; and liquids which will, magically, eliminate her own naturally disgusting odor and bestow, instead, a fragrance so enchanting that she will no longer be repellent to any man who, however repellent and boorish himself, might wish casually to seduce her. The seduction is an ordeal, otherwise humiliating, made rapturous by the bewitching compounds she has applied to her lips and teeth which momentarily entrance him and conjure in both his heart and his brain a wish, immediately indulged, to marry her. Once married, a woman's days are made sunny by her husband's desire for a white shirt, her children's demand for cereals, and, of course, her own continuing lust for miracles. Fortunately, there are plenty of miracles about. There is something magic to clean the bath; something occult to polish the floor; a flash of lightning sees to the washing up; a touch of sorcery produces food fit for a god; a little fairy leads her each day to the best buy in the supermarket; and a kindly gnome caresses away her headache.

Nothing agreeable, nothing even bearable, happens to a woman, it is suggested, except by magic; a magic, moreover, so subtle and uncanny that, though raised from the vast, mysterious deep by men, it is nevertheless invalid in their hands; although it is men who, indefatigably inquisitive, discover and proclaim the weird power contained in finely ground pumice, compressed ox blood, concentrate of ammonia and the like, it is only in the hands of women that the actual magic can be made manifest. It would be a ludicrous television advertisement that depicted a man attempting to clean a filthy dirty kitchen floor with a mop impregnated with beewax and turpentine, for no amount of sorcery on his part will reproduce from these substances the powers, other than those they quite naturally possess, with which he has so thoughtfully invested them. He would have to rub away at the floor for hours on end, and an utterly dispiriting sight that would be. The best he can do is to give—well, sell—the apparently ordinary floor polish, meat cubes, extract of malt, solution of alum, crushed oats, dilute carbolic acid, cow's milk and so on to women, fabulous beings, reverenced by the name "housewives" in the presence and at the touch of whom, uniquely, these mundane materials put forth their wizardry. Thus does margarine become indistinguishable from butter, drudgery from ease, misery from happiness and existence from life.

It is all done by magic; woman's magic—that is manmade television's message. And the awful thing is that Englishwomen believe it. They seriously imagine that there is about them a little touch of magic which makes the feminist's battle on their behalf quite unnecessary, not to say pushy and vulgar. Why bother to claim that one is as capable of thought and of rational action as a man when one can, with less exertion, work miracles? It is a pity, of course, that such things as railway trains, riots, coal-heaving, the disposal of sewage, micro-biology, politics, war, flood, and famine are not susceptible to her miracles, but still, these are superficial matters and in any case a woman can banish them in a way, any time she feels like it, since she has only to cast one of her several spells to make a man entirely oblivious of them. Oblivious, indeed, of everything, for a television husband changes from an alert human being into an obsequious zombie the moment she makes a couple of hypnotic passes with her day's magic charm, be it so simple as one she has used on him a hundred times before—a cup of instant coffee, say.

Why is it that Englishmen propagate so carefully the absurd and uncomplimentary notion that their women are magical? Can it simply be selfishness? Yes, it can. For once the women accept this alluring idea, they are, paradoxically, completely at the mercy of men! Just as the snake is mesmerized by the belief that *it*, by elevating itself, is producing the music from the charmer's pipe, so is the Englishwoman mesmerized by the belief that she, by performing various easy tricks, is controlling the world she lives in. But it is the man, as we know, who controls the supply of the magic wands without which a woman is merely human. If she does not behave herself properly, that is to say if she does not do exactly what she is told and expected by men to do, then she will not be given the money for her love filters and Aladdin's lamps, especially the more expensive and therefore more powerful ones. She will either have to do without, in which case she ceases to be a real magician, or else go herself and earn the money for them, in which case, of course, she ceases to be a real woman.

That most powerful magic object, the washing machine, is an excellent example. At first, one might imagine that this was designed to give women a measure of genuine freedom from the serf-pen, or kitchen, as it is called. Nothing of the sort. It is through the washing machine that Englishmen subjugate their womenfolk and keep their grip on "the English way of life." Mind you, they had a very narrow escape. For a few desperate moments it looked as though the washing machine, so simple and effective, really would free women. Then, in the nick of time, men thought of associating with it the properties, long since known to them in their industries, of detergents. And Englishwomen have been knocking themselves out ever since, stuffing their enameled whirligigs with load after load after load of inconspicuously soiled clothing and domestic linen, then drying it, and then ironing it, all as a prelude to trying to decide which of their magic substances washes whitest, a question which men, laughing meanwhile up their gleaming shirtsleeves, can safely leave to women since it is a wholly spurious problem of no more real consequence than whether the snake charmer's music is melodious. It is noticeable that the "unreal" women of England—the women, so reviled by Englishmen, who are emancipated enough to think of themselves first as human beings and only secondly as female—do with their dirty washing exactly what the men do. They send it to a laundry—a real one that they have to pay, it's true—and get on themselves with something, surely not difficult to imagine, more interesting and more important.

Any investigation and criticism of the Englishwoman is fundamentally a criticism of the Englishman, of course, and there is little hope for any change in her status and outlook so long as there is no modification of his. That the women are vaguely aware and envious of a larger, freer life is demonstrated by their admiration of female film stars and members of the Royal Family and high society; they are not fascinated by their wealth and fame so much as by their freedom. But as long as men are running England, they will conspire to keep their women in subjection as cooks, cleaners, and baby sitters, allowing them the consolation that every great civilization has been based on a slave population—Babylon, Greece, Rome—or on something very close to it, such as the serfdom of renaissance Italy, or the exploited laborers and the army of domestic servants in nineteenth century England. In the bright civilization of England as the twentieth century draws to its close, women have the comfort of knowing that, but for them and the leisure created by their servitude, we would never have witnessed the glories of Panorama,

Harlow New Town and The Kinks, by which an admiring and grateful posterity will remember us.

What is so striking is that even the younger generation of Englishwomen, the most famously "emancipated" and swinging girls in all the world, appear in fact to be falling in their millions into the same trap as their mothers. For their favorite fashions are those, notably the mini-skirt, which most decisively reveal and proclaim their ability to function as what they delight in being called: dollies. Which is to say inert, man-made, brainless, entirely complaisant toys, useful for the age-old game of mothers and fathers and nothing else.

Love and marriage: the twin obsessions of Englishwomen of all ages. A recent poll, in which they were asked what was their fondest hope and ambition, disclosed that 95% wanted a happy marriage. The fact that 63% were already married says a great deal, and none of it complimentary, about their spouses.

9

Figures
of Authority

THERE once was a good and kindly man called Harold Mackintosh who used to make and sell every year hundreds of tons of toffees, bulls' eyes, sherbet dabs, licorice bootlaces, jelly babies, and other sorts of candy. He was well thought of in his own small world of confectionery manufacturers, and by little children everywhere. He could have lived a life of comfortable obscurity, had he not been so clever at selling candy that he became rich and important enough to be a distinguished Baron, in 1948, and, rather better, a Viscount, in 1957.

In this quaint way, England bred a superlative example of that which England alone can breed well—a Figure of Authority.

A Figure of Authority is a person who possesses the pure, distilled essence of authority; he is revered and respected for what he appears to be, rather than what he actually is or what he actually has done. He *may* be knowledgeable and experienced—Harold Mackintosh knew all one could wish to know about a child's perfectly natural taste for toffee apples—but neither wit nor wisdom is essential. Only the ability never to have been wrong; and that *is* a matter of ability, not of luck, for the ability never to have been wrong consists of the ability never to have tried, too heatedly, to be right. A Figure of Authority is a person who has always avoided uttering words, or taking action, that contained an element of risk. Avoided, in fact, all positive statements and actions; refrained from advocating any new cause; searched always for areas of agreement, however small, minimized always the significance of areas of disagreement, however large. A Figure of Authority has been passionate about nothing, never gone to extremes, disturbed no stone that could decently be left unturned.

This being so, you can easily imagine that in all the whole wide range of human activity there is nothing more innocent, more inoffensive, more tolerable than making jelly babies. Harold Mackintosh, consistently offering the public something nice to suck, had had no occasion to upset anyone. Let other men cry out for a strong pound, his modest claim was always for a strong penny, clutched in a sticky little hand. Let other men raise a flag and call on the people to follow, he merely gave them something to chew while they thought about it.

We have in England any number of authority organizations. There is the White Fish Authority, the Electricity Authority, the National Environment Research Council, the Thames Conservancy Board, the Cheadle and Gatley Urban District Council, the Institute of Arbitrators, the

Government, etc. etc. etc. And each of these authorities occasionally needs a Figure of Authority through whom it can speak to us and tell us what we ought to do and what we ought not to do; when to pull our socks up and when to let our hair down; and whether we are trying hard enough. A dependable, unchanging, above all authoritative Big Daddy.

One such authority is the Advertisers' Association. This is an organization dedicated to the proposition that we should all be made to spend our money as fast as we possibly can. Fork over! That is the message of the Advertisers' Association. And for a long while, the Figure of Authority through whom they barked it at us was Viscount Mackintosh.

Another such authority is the National Savings Committee. This organization is dedicated to the proposition that we shall all be made to spend our money as slowly as we possibly can. Save up! That is the message of the National Savings Committee. And for a long while, their Figure of Authority was the same Viscount Mackintosh.

And the most important part of this tale is that Viscount Mackintosh was President of one authority and Chairman of the other at exactly the same time! It did not matter a bit. He was no longer a sweet maker, or a spender, or a saver. He was a Figure of Authority.

"Dost thou know me, fellow?" said King Lear to the Earl of Kent.

"No, Sir, but you have that in your countenance which I would fain call Master."

"What's that?" asked Lear.

"Authority," replied Kent, thereafter following and obeying him.

When he was appointed Chairman of the Governors of the B.B.C., Lord Normanbrook was placed in a curious position. Having spent the best part of his professional life as Secretary to the Cabinet with the job of trying to conceal information, he was suddenly Chairman of an organization charged with the discovery and dissemination of it by professional and technical means of which he knew nothing. The features of Sir Basil Smallpiece were thought extraordinarily compelling when, as Chairman of the British Overseas Airways Corporation, he told us we had best go by air; they are no less urgent now that, as Chairman of the Cunard Steamship Company, he exhorts us to go by sea. Sir Harry Pilkington's sublime air was sufficiently authoritative for the chairmanship of a Government Committee on television, though his only personal connection with the whole complex business was that his firm makes most of the glass we see it through.

Figures of Authority all, suitable for any bit of business.

The best way to understand what authority means to us today is to look at intellectual authority, especially in the scientific subjects. As science gets more and more complicated, and at the same time touches our lives at more and more points, it becomes impossible for more than a handful of people to weigh the evidence for a scientific assertion and decide if it is right, or even reasonable. Does butter cause coronary thrombosis? Is plastic as strong as leather? Which way to the moon? Should we sleep on the right side or the left? Can diesel fumes cause cancer? How did the world begin? When *will* pigs fly? We would all like to understand these weighty matters, but, failing that, we would at least like to know. Does it, or doesn't it? Will it or won't it? Can it or can't it? Yes or no? And to our simple questions, authorities give forthright answers. But our choice is not really between ignorance and knowledge; it is between ignorance and the illusion of knowledge. Do we *know* that there is a dollar gap, or even that the world is round? Not at firsthand. We wait for an authority to tell us. The same sort of authorities who said World War I would last eight weeks. For the awful fact is that authority itself is sometimes illusory; indeed, it is often plain wrong, though it hates ever to admit it.

Doctor James J. Walsh—and doctors are all stupendously imposing authorities—announced to a gratified New York on January 7, 1900, that the horseless carriage, the automobile, was about to confer inestimable benefit upon mankind. Everybody realized, of course, that it was going to enable them to get quickly from one place to another, but what so inspired the doctor about the horseless carriage was that it would give the common housefly such a hard time. He brought many facts and figures and such sound argument in proof of his assertion, which was greatly talked about and enthused over by other scientists at the time.

"Insects," said Doctor James J. Walsh, "have their

favorite places for laying eggs. These places are carefully chosen. The butterfly *seems* to circle around and light on any flowers. As a matter of fact, he goes to one particular flower. These things are never the result of chance. Now, it is a *scientific fact* that the common housefly lays his eggs in horse manure. In this, the eggs flourish prodigiously. With the horse off our streets, the fly must follow him. It will not be where the horse is not. Thus, a serious channel of infection will be done away with and many lives spared. The horseless carriage will greatly reduce the death rate in cities."

Everyone accepted this authoritative statement, except the common housefly, which still seems to be circulating around, lighting here and there, laying its eggs and spreading infection. Meanwhile, the horseless carriage, also flourishing prodigiously, is killing us off like flies.

Another example of scientific authority is this, taken from a most imposing book telling us how to keep fit and strong; "Standing balanced on the right leg, raise the other one to the side as high as you can. Grasp the instep with the right hand and extend the other leg, raising the opposite hand with palm up in a graceful position." What the book *should* have said is, "extend the other leg, then get someone to pull it." Anyhow, if you are determined to try this authoritative exercise, please wave good bye, gracefully, with palm up, as they carry you away.

Wave especially, to Sir Hugh Munro-Lucas-Tooth of Teanenich, emphatically a Figure of Authority, given to speaking his mind on all manner of topics, who is on the record with: "If hydrogen bombs are exploded all over this country, it could transform our whole way of life." And salute the clergyman in Newcastle who announced firmly, "We must bring back the death penalty in order to emphasize the sanctity of human life."

Above all, blow a kiss to Sir Thomas Padmore, a very senior Civil Servant who has learned well the lesson that he need never be right so long as he is never obviously wrong. Giving evidence to the Royal Commission on the Civil Service, he said: "What I have said has demonstrated that it is very difficult to find an answer to that question; but, if I were pressed for an answer, I would say that, so far as we can see, taking it rather by and large, taking one time with another, and taking the average of Departments, it is probable that there would not be found to be very much in it either way."

He then, presumably, lighted on a flower and laid an egg. And if only he and people like him would go where the horse is not, a really serious channel of infection would be done away with and many lives spared, because the language of authority is more deadly than any common housefly.

"This is a Bill which has shocked the conscience of every Christian community in Europe," the Earl of Birkenhead once told a hushed House of Lords. He was referring to a measure which conferred a mild autonomy upon Christian community in Wales, and what the Earl of

Birkenhead really meant was that it might upset him and a few of his friends. Authority tries to protect its position by the language it uses, which never means what it says.

"The matter is under consideration" means "We have lost the file."

"The matter is under active consideration"—"Someone is trying to find the file."

"It is not in the public interest"—"It is in the public interest, but not ours."

"Public opinion is not yet ready for such a step"—"The public is ready but we are not."

"This is an urgent problem and we are therefore setting up a Royal Commission"—"This is terrible, but we hope that in three years either everyone will have forgotten all about it or we can find someone else to blame."

"As I said at the last annual meeting, this remains an important, indeed vital, part of the company's policy, but there is, unfortunately, no immediate opportunity of implementing it"—"Forget it."

"In the fullness of time"—"Never."

"In the not too distant future"—"Never."

"Never"—"As soon as we dare."

"We have had a full, frank and far-ranging exchange of views and both governments look forward to meeting again at a later date"—"We are at war."

"We are regrouping our forces for a final successful attack"—"The Cabinet is leaving London."

A "strategic withdrawal" is a rout, a "phased withdrawal" is a rout with insufficient transport. A "deliberate, unprovoked act of aggression" is their side starting a war; "a pre-emptive air strike" is our side starting a war. The original pre-emptive air strike having taken place some years ago at Pearl Harbor. Though that was their side.

But although Authority often expresses itself through its figures, it prefers on the whole to work anonymously. "The local authority has decided that. . . . The Treasury ruling is. . . . The Regional Group Headquarters require. . . . The subcommittee has concluded. . . ." And with good reason. For these designations have a ring of authenticity which does not attach, individually, to any of the bigots and reprobates who together compose them. If we knew the actual men who made the decisions; knew their total human inadequacy; their addiction to whisky and dyed blondes; their driving habits; their abysmal taste in socks; if, in short, they ever betrayed that they are just like the rest of us, we would never take their rulings seriously. People who wield authority are usually blood-brothers of the man who was needed as a witness at Middlesborough police court, and of whom a lawyer, asking that he should be excused attendance, said, "In the first place, he is not of very bright intellect. Secondly, he is employed on important Government work."

Anonymity encourages authority to behave with a degree of stupidity and cruelty quite alien to human beings. No *person* would dock a schoolmistress half a day's pay after giving her the afternoon off so that she could be presented with a medal for risking her life to save a child from drowning. But the Inner London Education Authority did. And, even after a public outcry, it took six months to decide to refund it. Similarly, Peterborough Rural Council demanded four weeks' rent in lieu of notice when Mrs. Minnie Day "vacated a council bungalow without forwarding the statutory four weeks' notice." Mrs. Day had, in fact, died. The council, knowing this, sent its demand to her next-of-kin. They probably paid up, since authority tends to be so awesome we quite often submit to it in the belief, or at least faint hope, that it must in some way be for our own good, and the thought that perhaps after all principle and authority are not mutually exclusive. But, alas, they are. Look at Labor, or immigration, or Vietnam. Authority is busy preventing disturbance, keeping things quiet, tiding over and all the apparatus of pragmatism: it is the force which destroyed Antigone and St. Joan. Its watchword is not just "right" or "liberty" or "justice"; it is "consensus."

What must always be remembered is that people in high places want to stay in high places. This, indeed, is authority's closest concern. If the purpose for which an authority was formed clashes with the preservation of that authority, then the purpose goes to the wall. Trade unions, for example, were formed to get better conditions for their members. But if those members lay down their tools against the advice of their union officials, then the officials side with the employer in deploring an "unofficial strike." The official argument (never openly expressed) is: "On the one hand, our authority is being defied. On the other hand, we are betraying the purpose for which our authority was established. But, whereas if we betray our purpose we might be able to redeem ourselves later, if we lose our authority, we lose it for ever. Therefore we must fight to preserve our authority, and betray our purpose."

The worst offense then, is to defy authority. In court you can be sent to jail for an unlimited time without trial and without appeal if you simply say "I won't" to the judge. For murder, rape, treason and other minor offenses, you are granted the full processes of the law, but for the defiance of authority, the thought is not entertained for a moment.

Fanatically, stupidly, and to the very last ditch, authority will fight to maintain itself. A provincial newspaper recently reported: "Council workmen are to rip planks out of seats and make holes in the walls of bus shelters in an attempt to make the shelters too uncomfortable for hooligans. Councillor Harry Bill said: 'Something has got to be done to stop the wrecking of these shelters. So far as I can see, this is the only way.'"

Perhaps he was influenced by the Crown Lease which, granting someone the right to rent a fifth floor flat, contained a clause forbidding him to use it as a garage, or for the training or stabling of horses (no actual *mention* of the common housefly, but one sees what they vaguely had in mind). Or the authority that disqualified a schoolgirl swimmer from a championship race because she had only one leg, and therefore broke their rule that "legs must move simultaneously." Or the council that, commissioning a piece of sculpture called "Family Group" from Henry Moore, ordered him to leave no holes in which small boys could trap their heads. For authority, like everyone else, knows nothing about art, but it damned well knows what it likes—and what *we* will like.

But how do you deal with authority? Big game hunters say that if you encounter a lion in the jungle, you are perfectly safe if you advance on it slowly but steadily, making sure all the time that it has a safe line of retreat. Corner it and it will kill you, or at least make a mess of your self-respect. So with authority. It, too, in a face-to-face encounter, is a fierce, man-eating animal and must be treated as such.

But of course, face-to-face encounters are rare. On the whole, we are the ones who feel cornered and look anxiously over our shoulders for a safe and not too un-dignified line of retreat. After all, we are taught quite early, first, that conflict is best avoided; second, that if it is inevitable, submission is the better part of valor. "Write out a hundred times, 'I must learn to think for myself,' " as our teachers arrange it, with such indelicate irony. Thus, we learn to accept authority and lose all desire to quarrel with it. Even the Bible, we recall, has inscribed on its title page the simple words, "Published by Author-ity." In a strange and bewildering world, we gradually find we *need* authority—we are lost without the comfort and reassurance that it seems to provide. Why, even the Dartmoor Prisoners Debating Society passed by a large majority a resolution asking for the re-introduction of corporal punishment and hanging.

We in our turn will more or less happily swallow all sorts of rubbish, rub in any manner of agony, on the grounds that, "Well, the doctor [or the pharmacist, or the dietician, or the man in the newspaper, or the wart curer, etc. etc.] says it's good for me." One or another—or several —of these authorities told us that thalidomide was a perfectly safe drug. Perhaps that is the most acute recent example of scientific authority confounded, but we can be quite sure there are many others. If only we knew which they were! What else are they telling us to do that is going to turn out all a terrible mistake? And which authority, when two apparently equal bodies differ between themselves, should we follow? If one authority says the pill will cause blood clots and another says it won't, what are we to do?

This sort of fight between lions would be very upsetting if it were not for television, which manages the controversy for us. For what happens when authorities fall out is that representatives of both sides are invited to a studio for a discussion. Since none of us viewers are equipped to understand or evaluate the arguments on either side, the actual dispute is often simplified into near-meaninglessness, and what we are then invited to judge between is the personal appeal of the representatives. If the pro-pill chap seems to be humorous, cheerful, and down to earth, and the anti-pill chap is prickly, tight-lipped and arrogant, we will decide the pill is all right. Reverse the roles, and we reverse our conclusions. They have nothing to do with reason or fact, or science. Simply that, if we have to choose between one authority and another, we prefer that which seems nicer, more comfortable, more like us. Yet, did we but know it, they would *both* agree to hang us up by our ears if we decided to challenge the *pair* of them!

It is said that somewhere in England there is a man who challenges all authority. He keeps his Milk of Magnesia in a hot place. When the radio says, "Turn the lights down low, it's time for dancing," he turns the lights up high and goes to bed. When the notice of a transmission breakdown flashes on the television screen, he always adjusts his own set; on the other hand, he never adjusts his clothing before leaving. He buys instant coffee, then makes it slowly. During the second chorus, he doesn't join in. Rather than go to work on an egg, he eats cheese for breakfast and has given up his job. He writes in all spaces marked "Reserved for official use." He reads instructions carelessly, although if a jar label says, "Pierce lid and push off," he will certainly pierce it, but then he stays right where he is. He sends money now, accepts substitutes, handles clumsily, remembers his troubles, underacts his age, thinks small, keeps his chin down, and does his worst. Moreover, he does it later.

Such a man would have felt challenged by the notice on the Yorkshire moors which announced, quite simply, "It is forbidden to throw stones at this notice."

It sums up so much of authority—stupid, arrogant, pointless and, secretly, rather afraid of *us*.

10

The Religion of Medicine

WHILE the English have their own peculiar adherence to sin, they do at least balance it with a peculiar adherence to religion, a new religion.

Voltaire said that the art of medicine consists of amusing the patient while nature cures the disease. But he was a Frenchman. There is nothing amusing about the practice of medicine in England. It is a deeply serious matter. Fifty or sixty years ago, pain and misery were a valuable part of our way of life and it was an Englishman's lot to stand them without flinching. Treatment was endurable only if it was unbearable; the agony of iodine and the filthiness of castor were permitted, but other than that an Englishman gritted his teeth and soldiered on. Only the weakest went to the medicine cabinet. It was just one of his many, many duties and a fine example to weaker and lesser breeds everywhere.

The age of affluence has changed all that, for pleasure, rather than duty, is now our watchword. Pain is no longer regarded as something worthwhile, something to teach an Englishman to endure the cold of the South Pole to win glory for the Union Jack, or to withstand the burning sun and the sucking leeches as he strode through the African swamps on his way to hold court in the next village, or to stick it out in Flanders mud and the Dunkirk beach until deliverance or death. Pain, now, is simply something that hurts.

Co-incidental with this change in the English attitude toward pain has been a tremendous increase in the availability of palliative and curative drugs. Sulfonamides, penicillin, barbiturates—one after another they have appeared in the doctor's office and on the pharmacy's shelves. Although some of these new drugs seem to be so strong that one must be in perfect health to take them. Nevertheless, they have undermined the healthy skepticism of the old days, when even the most ignorant layman could see that doctors were little more refined than butchers, and we now believe that doctors can actually cure us.

There may not be many housemaids left to have knee, or top athletes left to have foot, and in the new era the great threat may turn out to be one-armed bandit's elbow and complex contusions of the forefinger caused by trying to reach Barcelona on a long distance dial phone, but there is no doubt that with more and more fashionable phrases like "virus infection" and "slipped disc" to impress the uninitiated, the doctor in his power over his patients is closer to the medicine man than he has been this century. So strong is the English belief in him that they now have what they call "established health"—the National Health Service—at the center of the new religion to which, ignoring Voltaire and nature, they have handed themselves over body and soul. (English doctors themselves are well aware of this, and in one respect resentful of it. Elsewhere in the world, they see their brethren getting richer and richer, while they have to stay comparatively poor. For they are our new priesthood and the English, unlike other people, particularly Continentals and Americans, do not believe in wealthy priests. They demand poverty as a proof of saintliness.)

It is to doctors that the English now submit when they feel they should do penance—"No smoking, no rich food and take plenty of exercise"—and when they seek indulgences for sins not yet committed—"Yes, you can stay home from the job for three days." And doctors now hear so many confessions in their offices that a kneeling pad and a grille would often be of more use than an examination table. That is why everyone was so particularly furious about Lord Moran and his diaries. He had broken the oath not of the doctor's office but of the confessional. The medical profession has taken over from the clergy the arrangements for all the central events of our lives. Weddings are solemnized not in church with a ring, but in family planning clinics with a coil; post-natal clinics replace baptismal ceremonies; and the catechism for pubescent children to prepare them for confirmation has given way to sexual instruction to prepare them for copulation. Family prayers are replaced by rose hip syrup and cod liver oil, and tablets and medicines usurp the bread and wine. The doctor gets all the reverence once reserved for the vicar, a fact made clear by this report from *The Sun:* "A husband suffering from flu saw the doctor, who had just visited him, kiss his wife at the foot of the stairs. The husband 'under great provocation' nearly hit him with a milk bottle. But, out of respect for the doctor's profession, he refrained and punched his wife instead."

Although an Englishman used to care naught for his body, at least he took good care to know his own mind, but now he even gives that, along with his slipped disc and virus infection, into the safe keeping of his medical practitioner. Where once he was either brave or cowardly, generous or mean, energetic or lazy, and needed strength of character to overcome his weaknesses, now he is merely maladjusted, and the cure is not guts but a trip to the doctor. The seven deadly sins are simply forms of psychological disturbance: pride is egomania, lust is sexual deprivation, envy is obsessional neurosis, covetousness is fear of loss, gluttony is an affection-want transference, wrath is insecurity sublimation, and sloth is social defense mechanism. And the doctor or psychiatrist can do something about all of them—or at least you cannot prove they can't. In the words of one London physician, "We got to him just in time—another two days and he would have recovered without us."

THE RELIGION OF MEDICINE

Faith is important: very few Englishmen today are impious enough to blaspheme in the terrible way of the man who wrote to the *Daily Telegraph* saying: "I venture to think ailments run in fashions. Thirty years ago one had one's appendix out; twenty years ago one had to have all one's teeth out; now the fashion is slipped disc and lung cancer. I do not believe in lung cancer and hope these scares will soon die down." Though of course the great strength of the clergy has always been that they were estate agents for the Elysian Fields: only through them could you acquire a small holding in Paradise. Now that people no longer believe in life after death, it is hardly surprising if the fashion is for them to devote more and more of their care and thought to life before death, to maximum pleasure and minimum pain during it, and to prolonging it as much as possible. It is not the Devil who is now the dreaded enemy, it is liver trouble and lung trouble and heart trouble. The cigarette and the cream bun are the Satanic temptations of today, and the diets, health farms, gymnasia, the daily exercises and deep breathing, the regular weighing, the small cigars, starch-reduced rolls, and sugar substitutes are the rituals of the new English religion.

Of course, there are heresies and schisms—osteopathy, acupuncture, vegetarianism—but the underlying beliefs are the same. These worshippers may murmur different spells at different shrines, but they are fighting the same enemies, pain and death, in truly ecumenical fashion.

The doctors, like the clergy of old, use people's fears

to extort money from them, not now for missions to Africa but for "medical research." As in all faiths, the religion of medicine has a hierarchy—from humble monks and nuns (hospital orderlies and nurses, some in enclosed orders—hospitals—and some wandering ones—visiting nurses) through the main body of the church, formed by general practitioners; to cardinals and bishops (senior specialists and consultants) and finally such canonized saints as Fleming, Pasteur, Schweitzer and the Curies. Their prescriptions, naturally, are written in Latin. There are many learned works for the clergy, but only one Good Book for the masses—Doctor Spock. Anyone who lets the faith down can be unfrocked (struck from the Medical Register), and both new and old religions regard adultery with a follower as a heinous sin, punishable by immediate expulsion, as though it were somehow morally worse for a doctor than for a greengrocer to commit adultery with a customer.

The new religion, just like the old, panders to hopes and trades on fears. Which points to an obvious conclusion—a merger. England has overworked doctors and under-occupied clergymen; over-full hospitals and empty churches; and a completely duplicated staff at every level. Priests could take over a big proportion of doctors' cases, for at least half the patients want someone to talk to more than anything else; though since they will only talk freely in the right medical atmosphere, we would need to replace the hymn sheets with temperature and pulse charts, and the church pews with rows of beds and screens and perhaps a little additional heating.

The English would benefit greatly if this suggestion was adopted, but there is, unfortunately, an insurmountable obstacle to it. The merger is dictated by reason, but opposed by emotion. And since both clergymen and doctors owe their power to the dominance of human emotion over human reason, both will fight it to the death.

11

It
Pays to
Advertise

ONE OF the most authoritative voices speaking to us today is, of course, the voice of the advertisers. Its strident clamor dominates our lives. It shouts at us from the television screen and the radio loudspeaker; waves to us from every page of the newspaper; plucks at our sleeves on the escalator; signals to us from the roadside billboards all day and flashes messages to us in colored lights all night. It has forced on us a whole new conception of the popular man as a man less than 20% of whose mail consists of announcements of giant carpet sales.

Advertising has been among England's biggest growth industries since the war, in terms of the ration of money earnings to demonstrable achievement. Why all this fantastic expenditure?

Perhaps the answer is that advertising saves the manufacturers from having to think about the customer. At the

stage of designing and developing a product, there is quite
enough to think about without worrying over whether any-
body will want to buy it. The designer is busy enough
without adding customer-appeal to all his other problems
of man-hours and machine tolerances and stress factors. So
they just go ahead and make the thing and leave it to the
advertiser to find eleven ways of making it appeal to purchasers after they have finished it, by pretending that it
confers status, or attracts love, or signifies manliness. If the
advertising agency can do this authoritatively enough, the
manufacturer is in clover.

Other manufacturers find advertising saves them
changing their product. And manufacturers hate change.
The ideal product is one which goes on unchanged forever. If, therefore, for one reason or another, some altera-
tion seems called for—how much better to change the
image, the packet or the pitch made by the product, rather
than go to all the inconvenience of changing the product
itself.

The advertising man has to combine the qualities of
the three most authoritative professions: Church, Bar, and
Medicine. The great skill required of our priests, most
highly developed in missionaries but present, indeed
mandatory, in all, is the skill of getting people to believe
in and contribute money to something which can never
be logically proved. At the Bar, an essential ability is that
of presenting the most persuasive case you can to a jury
of ordinary people, with emotional appeals masquerading

as logical exposition; a case you do not necessarily have to *believe* in yourself, just one you have studiously avoided discovering to be false. As for Medicine, any doctor will confirm that a large part of his job is not clinical treatment but faith healing. His apparently scientific approach enables his patients to believe that he knows exactly what is wrong with them and exactly what they need to put them right, just as advertising does—"Run down? You need. . . ." "No one will dance with you? A dab of— will make you popular."

Advertising men use statistics rather like a drunk uses a lamp-post—for support rather than illumination. They will dress anyone up in a white coat to appear like an unimpeachable authority or, failing that, they will even be happy with the announcement, "As used by 90% of the actors who play doctors on television." Their engaging quality is that they enjoy having their latest ruses uncovered almost as much as anyone else.

Their ruses are easy enough to uncover. Squadron Leader Barclay, complaining about them in a letter to a newspaper, said: "Why do advertisers continually announce '17% more' without adding 'than what?' A few months ago I wrote to a well-known tire company whose advertisements announced 'twice the grip, twice the mileage.' I asked, 'The grip and mileage of what?' and added that I had invented a rubber with 847 times the grip and 943 times the mileage, but as my basic test piece was a banana, I doubted whether I had a commercial proposition."

[145]

Very few people would ever advocate a ban on advertising—it is too valuable as a lubricant for society. But what is needed is a constant intelligence service to outline all the latest tricks in the game, so that people do not get too excited by offers which end up like that "bathing suit 50% off" which turned out to be topless, and the "simple and elegant coathanger" which turned out to be a nail. In short, somebody needs to be appointed to remind everybody regularly that "Amazing offer" means "Send ten shillings for a five shilling steak knife" and "Free" means "Not enough people sent ten shillings for a five shilling steak knife."

Of course, the advertiser needs help to get his message across to the public. He turns to artists—on an unprecedented scale—to provide it. Never has there been so much demand for the artist's gifts, never so little for his personal vision of the truth. Not only do many actors and writers and journalists depend indirectly upon advertising to support the medium in which they earn their living, but a huge number of truly creative people find that the best money comes from advertising, and so it is to advertising that they go. Photographers try to graduate to advertising; painters and graphic artists and illustrators pour out from art schools every year and into advertising agencies; film directors depend on commercials between films; composers and orchestras devote much of their creative lives to twenty second jingles.

Not that there is anything wrong in principle with

artists receiving money from the rich to do what the rich want. It was, after all, the Emperor Augustus who got Virgil to write the history of the firm. During the Renaissance there was no conflict between good art and commercial art. There was a clear market price and the better the practitioner, the higher the price he commanded. So today's artist, entering a commercial world like advertising, can claim a distinguished set of precedents. But there is another reason, in addition to cash, why advertising is successful in luring so many artists into its fold. It is the development of coterie art: art which seems, to most people and many artists, to have no relation to life. Look, they say, at the situation today. Painting has completely taken leave of reality; nobody understands a word of modern poetry; sculptors invite art collectors and scrap metal dealers to their exhibitions, and then sell to the highest bidder; music is indistinguishable from a sound effects track made in a stone mason's yard; and architecture has standardized on the single-slab office-block. Nobody understands what art is, nobody has any standards by which to judge if art is good or bad—except possibly that of the Emperor and his new clothes, as exemplified by Sir Roland Penrose writing in *The Observer* about Picasso: "Emptiness has become very significant, the form, though not there, is there." While the coterie automatically rules out a poet if more than five hundred people buy his poems, the coterie artist himself rather resembles the English dons in America, described by Dylan Thomas as "lecturing on the rebirth of surrealism to an audience who did not know it was dead, never having known it was alive." Or, as the *Daily Mail* once said, "The fundamental good sense and decency of the English are rejecting decisively all attempts by television to give them what is loosely called 'culture'."

Little wonder then that many modern artists are trying to express themselves in new ways. Of course they meet with opposition, because of the traditionalist view that art must be where art always was, that the form which it used to take is the form which it must always take. Yet in Shakespeare's time, nobody thought of plays as an art form; in Jane Austen's time nobody believed the novel was art; even in Charlie Chaplin's time, nobody thought of his films as art. It is a little frightening to think that one day there may be, in addition to a Poet Laureate, a Potter Laureate or a Cereal Package Designer Laureate, but it could happen.

12

Managing the News

EVERYONE knows what news is. It is whatever happens in the world which is of importance or of interest. Just as well known is the fact that the English are so keen to be well-informed about what is going on that they buy and read more newspapers than any other people in the world. Their powerful and fearless newspaper industry is augmented by two competitive television channels and a national radio network, which between them fill in any conceivable gap left by the morning, evening, provincial, and week-end newspapers. Furthermore, ever since printing was invented, the English have fought for and won complete freedom for their press, so that there are no restraints on what they can read and hear and see. "The newspaper," as C. P. Scott of the *Manchester Guardian* said, "is of necessity something of a monopoly, and its first duty is to shun the temptations of monopoly. Its primary office is the gathering of news. At the peril of its soul it must see that the supply is not tainted. Neither in what it gives, nor in what it does not give, nor in the mode of presentation, must the unclouded face of truth suffer wrong. Comment is free, but facts are sacred."

So much for what we all know. Now for what every journalist knows, which is more or less the opposite. There are in fact so many restraints on what news the English may actually be given each day that it is the quite genuine achievement of the press that anything gets published at all.

To start with, there is the law of libel. If this meant simply that what was not true and might be damaging to someone could not be printed, the law of libel would be wholly beneficial. Unfortunately, it means also that what is true, and in the public interest to publish, cannot be printed unless the editor is confident he can get witnesses to go into court if necessary and tell the truth. He needs also a proprietor with the courage of his editor's convictions. And the more powerful and rich the people being written about, the greater is the required degree of confidence and courage. That is why everyone—everyone except the public—knew that a Cabinet Minister had compromised the government months before a word about his affair with the Russian naval attache's girl friend appeared in print. If the danger to security was as obvious and pressing as the papers later maintained, one might have expected them to draw public attention to it as soon as theirs had been. But they could not, or at any rate they did not, simply because of the libel laws. The best they could manage was innuendo by juxtaposition—placing news about "missing witness" Christine Keeler next to news or speculation about Mr. John Profumo's career. This was a technique which did nothing for the facts that C. P. Scott was going on about but did at least introduce the English publications' great new party game: that of finding other sinister positions like the recent—"Kings Road Dollies in Four Hour Orgy," "Duke of Gloucester at Chelsea Flower Show"—which are now automatically believed on the grounds that they must be true since the press has not published them in any other form.

Next, there is the danger of a newspaper's being held in contempt of court because it has published something which might offend or obstruct the judicial processes. The effect of this is to filter off many of the important facts about a crime, from the moment it is committed until the moment someone is convicted of it, because publication of them might be held to influence the jury. Indeed, these are conditions which also apply to the Court of Appeal, presumably on the grounds that the judges themselves would be swayed from their right judgment by a center page feature in the *Mirror*.

Then there are the notorious "security guidance D notices," by means of which the government inhibits the press from publishing matter which, according to the government, would imperil the safety of the realm. Such a notice once forbade publication of pictures of a building at Hatfield, although it was well-known and clearly visible from England's main road, the A-1, along which foreign spies in their hundreds could motor if they wished. The same system of "guidance" had the effect of reducing to practically nil the publication of information about Blue Streak. Whether or not complete freedom would have imperiled security nobody will ever know, but the mismanagement and the spiraling cost would certainly have imperiled the government if the public had been told about it.

Another instrument for suppression of a vast amount of news is the Official Secrets Act. An official secret is more or less anything that Whitehall says is an official secret. It need not be something the "enemy" would like to know; indeed it might well be something he already knows. But perhaps Whitehall does not want him to know that Whitehall knows he knows. Or even if he does know, and Whitehall knows he knows, and he knows that Whitehall knows that he knows, Whitehall still might not want the public to know. Whitehall might believe, for example, that disclosure of some incompetence or mistake on its part, although of no further relevance to the safety of the realm, would nevertheless be dangerous because it might both shake the public's faith in Whitehall and encourage confidence in the "enemy." Thus, for all practical purposes, Whitehall equates the public with the "enemy." And thus the Civil Service uses the Official Secrets Act like stretch nylon to cover almost any folly.

But the law is not the only news filter. Nor is it the

most selective. Some innocent people have been asking lately why the press has only in the last year or two been so fearfully agitated about the need to modernize Britain. Surely, they ask, if we are in such a terrible plight now, the signs must have been there for observant journalists to notice years ago. Why did we not read disturbing stories *then* about the failure of England's industrial giants to tool up with modern plants, improve their labor relations, freshen up their management, stop overstaffing, improve their marketing techniques and their arrangements for exports? News of all these matters was there to be written about in the forties and fifties, and it was not merely in the public interest but actually a public duty for the press to tell the country about them. Why did they not do so? The answer is down both sides of almost every page of every paper, every day. Advertising. It is not a question of pressure. It just introduces a hugely important new factor into making a judgment. Who is going to jeopardize the enormous sums of money paid out for advertising by Shell, or Dunlop, or Unilever, for the sake of what an editor can quickly convince himself, or be convinced of by the advertising manager, is a rather dull story anyway? Though few newspapers have gone as far as the *Argyllshire Advertiser,* which announced engagingly: "To avoid disappointing our advertisers a number of news items have had to be held over this week."

Another powerful agency for keeping the news out of the papers is any government minister. Even the English, who put up with a lot from their politicians, would not stand for a minister who got up in the House of Commons and said that such and such facts were so damaging to him and his colleagues in government that he had forbidden the press to publish them. What they have to stand for instead is the discretionary news system that enables a minister to talk to certain journalists "on a lobby basis." This beguiling phrase means that the minister will tell a paper's lobby correspondent any number of fascinating things—off the record. He may only publish those things the minister says he may publish and even those he cannot attribute in any way to the minister.

It is obvious that a correspondent who consistently ferrets things out for himself, particularly if they are nasty things, is not going to get much from the minister on a lobby, or any other, basis. The official hand-out will be his portion. No interesting leads or hints or tips for him. And he will find that his rivals on other papers are getting ten good stories—although none of them, of course, are uncomplimentary to the minister or the government—handed to them on a plate for every one he has had to dig out for himself. It is not surprising if he concludes that if he is going to get on with his editor he had better get on with the minister. Another advantage enjoyed by all men in high office is that they are well placed to hear all sorts of news and gossip quite unconnected with politics and the business of their departments. So they can exercise some control over the sort of news that is printed about themselves by controlling the tap from which they leak news about others.

The English press is far too free to allow anything like black lists of people or institutions, but there *is* such a thing as a proprietor's prejudice. It does not take an editor long to realize that it would be injudicious of him to publish a story praising a man who is consistently described by his employer as a stupid, useless, corrupt nincompoop. No black list is necessary; just a sensitive pair of ears. Lord Beaverbrook was always quite open, indeed raucous, about his likes and dislikes, so the public knew pretty well where they stood with him. But they could hardly be expected to detect a proprietor's prejudice from a list published in his paper of the numbers of visitors to England's stately homes. First on the list was Woburn Abbey, which belongs to the Duke of Bedford. Second was Longleat, home of the Marquess of Bath. In fact, more people visit Beaulieu than Longleat. But the paper's proprietor was prejudiced against the owner of Beaulieu, Lord Montagu, therefore his name did not appear. Almost all papers have unwritten rules of this sort.

And there is the editor's prejudice, which usually consists of the belief that he understands a situation better than the man he has sent, sometimes sent a long way at great expense, to look at it for him. At the time of Harold Macmillan's resignation, the political correspondent of one paper filed a story from the Conservative conference at Blackpool saying that the Conservatives would pick the

Earl of Home as their next leader. The editor, in London, was sure his man was wrong. He printed his story just as it was written, with the small exception that wherever Home was mentioned as successor he changed it to R. A. Butler.

Palace news is rarely the subject of straightforward suppression. The whole matter is instead kept on the plane of personal loyalty and gallantry and good form. And so the press will dutifully withold information of tremendous public interest which is being printed all over the world, and efforts are even made to censor incoming foreign periodicals and newspapers. Unless, that is, the rumor is both highly salacious and at the same time so utterly incredible as to be "safe," in which case one or other of the papers will peddle the vile rumor to its several million readers under the heading "This Paper Says! STOP PEDDLING THIS VILE RUMOR."

Even more, proprietors and editors both tend to exclude from the news discrediting stories about the press and the press barons themselves. The public and private lives of other tycoons are fair game, but not the public and private lives of prominent gentlemen of the press, whose private lives tend to be rather more entertaining than other people's. But dog does not bite dog—or son of a bitch eat son of a bitch, as Randolph would say—even if both are supposed to be watchdogs. Disputes in other industries are worth columns of space, but when nearly five million *Daily Mirror* readers are suddenly deprived of their paper one morning because of some dispute between the workers and the employers it merits no more than three or four lines in other papers.

Once all these filters have been used, what is left over can be considered for publication; which means it can be still further strained and reduced. The first qualification most stories have to meet is, did it happen today? For it is not sufficient for a story to be new, important, and interesting. It must also have happened today. Although this does not in the least matter to readers of news, it obsesses the writers and editors of it. They are deeply ashamed if they are absolutely forced to record something that happened yesterday. Television often has to invent "Today" stories in order to get in the day before's pictures. "Today Prince Charles spent the morning filling in the o's and e's in a copy of an Australian magazine following his arrival at Timbertop, where he had been greeted yesterday by cheering crowds and a pageant of English history put on by the senior boys." Much interesting news is thus excluded. Then, is there a picture of it? Of two stories, one may be more frivolous and insignificant than the other, but will nevertheless be given more space and prominence simply because the editor believes in having plenty of pictures in his paper, and there is a picture with the more frivolous story. This is particularly apparent in television news, in which fires, floods, and other pictorially dramatic events are reported to the exclusion of other news which is verbally stronger but visually weaker. Thus news stands a much

[157]

better chance if it happens within 30 miles of London or Manchester. Eagles in Regents Park get into the Press and onto television when two bears in the Isle of Wight never stand a chance. But even supposing that it happened today, and it is important, and there is a picture of it, it still faces another test: what *time* today did it happen? People who give out news, particularly politicians, know that time of day is a vital factor, so when possible, bad news is released just in time for the last editions of the evening papers. This leaves the editors of the dailies with the feeling that it is no use their giving it much space because everyone will have read it and been bored by it. Good news is released on Saturday mornings, because the Sunday papers are always eager for something besides sport to fill up their pages, and can be guaranteed to give it a good run. Something that happens after ten o'clock at night will not have been reported on the television news, and this gives it a special value; an intrinsically unimportant piece of news can easily displace something of consequence on the front page simply because it happened late at night and lends itself to a "midnight news" tag.

Then the question arises of who has reported the news. Newspapers are fed by news agencies, who send their stuff out impartially to everyone. If the agency story is very important everyone will print it. Otherwise, the night editor will prefer to use his space for stories from his own staff; even if their actual news value is lower than that of the agency reports, they have, for him at least, the merit of "exclusivity." Of course, the reader does not care two-pence if a story in his paper is also in another paper, but "exclusive" is a much prized tag in Fleet Street.

And one must not forget one of the most powerful filters of all—simply, whether or not the news gets to a journalist. We never find out about the vast majority of news which is never reported. Indeed it is fair to say that the amount of news that comes from any given region is in direct ratio not to the amount of "news" that happens but to the quantity (and quality) of journalists there. There are indeed any number of reasons why a story may not get through to the journalist. It may be the sort of city, Civil Service or industry story that would mean detaching four good reporters for six weeks with only a 50% chance of success. (There would be a battery of public relations men in attendance, requiring a similar number of press men on the other side to get at the truth.) The press often cannot afford this much manpower, and so the story that city, Civil Service, or industry really wishes to conceal can prove very elusive indeed. Or the obstacle to the journalist's getting the news can be a much more straightforward one. It may be simply that the journalist is looking for stereotype, and misses the story that does not fit into any of his categories. That the journalist will always be happy with a "£3000-a-year Company Director," whatever he is doing, or a £7-a-week, gray-haired and bespectacled mother of four who sits alone tonight and waits, and be absolutely delighted over raids with split-second timing, cats walking

[159]

200 miles to their old homes, and couples who have lived in the same house for 35 years (though they may have not spoken to each other for 34), but will miss totally the potential public interest to be found in "Man Savaged by Duck."

When a piece of news has finally passed through all the nets and filters and sieves already described, it has to win one last battle. The battle for space. Because quite apart from the machinery for keeping news out, there are several injectors for putting un-news in. Hence, all those articles on foreign countries, hedged around with advertisements for tourist agencies and airlines; and four-page reports on the car industry surrounded by advertising from car manufacturers. And un-news planted by public relations men—words and pictures about unknown but pretty actresses; words and pictures about a breakthrough in Swiss cheese or vegetable refrigeration; words and pictures about the profound pleasures of pipe smoking.

Every journalist is familiar with the P.R. man's "Now this really *is* news" which means "No it isn't" and his "I'm sorry old boy. No comment." which means "Now this really *is* news." Though it has to be admitted that sometimes journalists are tempted into creating un-news. It's so easy.

Then there are stories put in only to keep some important, highly-placed news source sweet; stories put in only to pacify some powerful person who was antagonized by a story printed the previous day; stories put in to publicize other companies in the same group as the newspaper; stories put in because top-line reporters and photographers have been somewhere at great expense and management has to be convinced that they are earning their money, even if the event they went to cover turns out to be boring or insignificant. If a piece of news wins this final battle, it is printed. The famous free press of England has done its job.

But can what the reader now buys now be described as newspapers? On an average day, no more than a quarter of the total space available in the paper he buys will have news printed on it. The remaining three-quarters will be occupied by advertisements, headlines, cartoons, features, comment, and such tabulated information as Stock Exchange prices and radio and television programs.

One can only conclude that newspapers are not so much devised and organized to disseminate news; news is devised and organized to disseminate newspapers. Perhaps it was his consciousness of all the problems involved that made newspaper tycoon Lord Rothermere say, when asked what his business was: "I buy wood pulp, process it, and sell it at a profit."

13

The
British
Government

FROM FAR and wide and every land they come to gaze in awe upon it—the seat of liberty, the throne of conscience, the cradle of democracy, the Mother of Parliaments. Here, beside the sweet Thames, if nowhere else in the world, a man can breathe the very air of freedom. Here, they are told, in this great Parliament, the people of England maintain to this day the right they established centuries ago to control their own destinies. This is the powerhouse; the very center of events; the model for constitutions which half the independent nations of Africa have overthrown. The visitor, suitably pious and humble, enters and mounts to the Strangers' Gallery. And what does he see? A few half-asleep Members of Parliament listening to one half-awake Member of Parliament making a speech, pausing every now and again for some piece of incomprehensible ritual as people in breeches, ruffles and

[163]

wigs strut in and out carrying symbolic sticks and baubles. That this Mother of Parliaments is a very ancient lady, not to say doddering, is confirmed to the visitor as it grows dark. In the gloom, he notices one of the lolling figures on the benches below uncoil itself and rise.

"Mr. Speaker," he says, plaintively, "I move that candles be brought in."

The electric lights are switched on. And the visitor departs, congratulating himself that he has done his duty but wishing he had chosen a day when something important was happening. He will hear later that a bill to make attendance at the House of Commons compulsory has been passed by three votes to two. He will think for a moment that one of the men he saw in the Chamber must have voted twice but then he will dismiss the thought from his mind and replace it, hopefully for England, with the fond and erroneous pre-conceptions with which he entered the Palace of Westminster.

Anyone who has actually been present in a place where matters of importance are discussed and decided knows that the atmosphere does not resemble that of a school debating society crossed with a Masonic lodge. But that is the atmosphere of Parliament. It is one of those English institutions—Trooping the Color, Changing the Guard, the Lord Mayor's Show, the Nottingham Goose Fair etc. etc.—in which the form remains enshrined in ceremony and tradition and ritual long after most of the substance has departed. There *was* real substance once. Parliament, after all, was the place where those who were going to be asked to pay taxes were summoned to make representations and give their advice about what taxes would be accepted and how they should be collected. There was even a time when it could refuse to allow the taxes. But once the political parties got Parliament sewn up a hundred years ago, with members having to submit to party discipline and party loyalty because it was party organization that got them into Parliament and kept them there, all power started to pass from Parliament to Government. And that is the way it has been moving ever since.

The consequence is that nine-tenths of what goes on at Westminster is an elaborate piece of play-acting. Most of the speeches are not intended to influence thought or action, but to enable members, through reports in their local newspapers, to prove to their constituents that they are still alive, if not omnipotent: to allow them to prove how hard they tried to stop the power station's being built in the city's only park. Even the much-vaunted Question Time is a piece of shadow boxing with rules carefully arranged so that nobody gets really hurt; a pantomime in which a Member flails a Minister with a bladder on a stick, and the Minister slaps back with a string of sausages. Thus: "Mr. James Dempsey (Labor, Coatbridge and Airdrie): to ask the Minister of Health, if, in the interests of hygiene, he will take steps to prohibit the practice of females wearing topless dresses in consuming establishments; and if he will make a statement."

"Mr. Snow. The Food Hygiene (General) Regulations, 1960, already provide a safeguard for hygiene by requiring food handlers to keep clean all parts of the person which are liable to come into contact with the food."

Parliament must make the most of its opportunities at Question Time because it is the only acknowledgment offered, however transparent, to its independence. The rest of the time, the Members are lobby fodder, rendered by the party system incapable of stopping, or even amending in any significant way, legislation of which they disapprove. Little wonder the more talented of their number begin to despair of the system. Proclaiming themselves in their campaign speeches as the people's watchdogs, they soon discover that they have no facilities whatever—no office, no secretary, no research teams—to enable them to keep watch in any serious way on the executive. All that is required of them as members of the country's sovereign assembly is that they shall vote as they are directed. A flicker of disobedience and they are hauled up to be ticked off by the whips; a serious sign of rebellion and the Prime Minister himself will lay into them with warnings that every dog is allowed one bite, but only one. At the second, its license is taken away; in other words the party withdraws its support.

They flex their muscles at Question Time, and then when the division bell rings they must meekly swallow whatever feelings of power this exercise has given them and, wiping the make-believe sweat from their brows, troop away behind their leader through the appropriate lobby door. Their choice is not between a sensible decision and a stupid decision, a good law or a bad one. It is between their party and the other party. Their mildest reservations, if pressed, are made a major issue of loyalty—not to good sense, not to good law, not even to the people they represent. But to the party.

The parties have cleverly contrived a system whereby backbenchers cannot stop measures they do not like when proposed by their own government—it is instantly a major issue of confidence, and instead of having to choose whether or not to let this one single measure become law, they have to choose whether to bring their whole government down, and perhaps precipitate a general election and let the other party in—perhaps even lose their seats as well. The consequence is that this has never been done, in this century anyway; M.P.'s have sometimes got rid of one leader and replaced him by another, sometimes dissolved or formed coalitions, but bring down their own government and force a general election—well, theoretically it could happen, just as, theoretically, the Queen could divorce Prince Philip and marry George Wigg.

Backbenchers with the right contacts among the press used to be able to exert some small influence on events by leaking advance information about plans to which they were opposed to newspapers which would also be opposed, and less inhibited about saying so. But even this activity is now denied them. Long since stripped of power, they now get no information either. The leaks became too frequent and now the information is decidedly scarce. Denial of power is being followed remorselessly by denial of information.

All this is not to say that Parliament does not serve a purpose; only that the purpose it serves is not that of the people, but of their rulers. It is very useful to the government as a barrier between the people and Whitehall. It serves as a safety valve; a place where the people can get things off their chests; a place for sound and fury signifying nothing. An angry Parliamentary debate has the same effect upon national events as a slammed door has upon domestic arguments. It is emphatic; it is deeply, though momentarily, satisfying; and it settles nothing at all. (Parliament consists, of course, of two Houses—Lords and Commons—but the House of Lords does not enter into the discussion at all. It has only two functions: to give out front row seats at Coronations, and to provide writing paper on which peers can write irate letters to the *Times* and placatory letters to tradesmen. Though of course on great matters of State it does have the constitutional right to say "Yes" or "Yes, but not for a few weeks." Recently it has tended to try to subordinate its frustrated political desires by continual discussions about sex.)

The difficulties Parliament finds in acting as any sort of representative voice of those who elect it can be seen by the recent growth of grass-roots organizations like Residents' Associations and Ratepayers' Associations. These bodies press directly, outside Parliament, for the reforms that they no longer hope their elected representatives can achieve, and they avoid any connection with any political party because they know that would mean death to their interests. The Consumers' Association is another of those bodies whose existence is proof of Parliament's ineffectiveness. It was to defend the people—as consumers and residents and ratepayers—that Parliament was instituted and members elected. Nowadays, however, such defense is in complete conflict with the all-consuming support that has to be rendered to their leaders.

It is at first sight surprising that such an institution should still be able to recruit members without conscription. But for one thing the pay is good (£3,000 a year and more if you are lucky, or particularly pliable). And for another the working hours are derisory. Although the constant cry of Parliament is that the country must work harder, it does not itself begin work until after lunch, never works on weekends and has three long holidays a year. Most of all, though, it offers that same prize which persuades so many of the English to become councilors and committee members and club secretaries—importance without great achievement, eminence without great effort. And some Members of Parliament are not frustrated by rigmarole and ritual. In fact they enjoy it, and view with complete equanimity a life of presenting chromium candlesticks to winning greyhounds and opening local fêtes as a last minute substitute for a starlet who has failed to turn up.

Mathematically that has to be the lot of the majority of

the 630 M.P.'s. There are only some twenty vital posts to fill—the key ministries—and another forty of considerable importance. The key question is: how are they to be selected?

To govern a highly complex, industrialized western nation of fifty-odd million people, the center of a turbulent commonwealth, one of the key signatories to a complicated web of pacts and treaties: supporting an international currency and providing one of the vital banking centers of the world; fighting to retain significant shipping, aircraft, automobile, computer, and machine tool industries in the face of fierce competition; sustaining one of the world's most comprehensive health services and trying to provide the sort of educational system that will be needed if the country is to compete at all in the seventies and eighties—to govern such a nation successfully demands consummate skill. It demands a deep study of the arts of government, a tough apprenticeship and lifelong experience in the actual problems at every level; and, at the top levels, a tenure of office that guarantees the continuity as well as the wisdom and understanding that are vital for long-term decisions and plans and negotiations. Look at the men who run Unilever and Standard Oil and General Motors—virtually all of them have served a long apprenticeship, faced a wide range of problems and achieved remarkable successes at higher and higher levels of management before finally being invited into the boardroom. Then look at the people who are going to run a far greater concern—the United Kingdom.

Obviously, their suitability for the tremendously exacting tasks before them calls for a rigorous examination to exclude all but those of the highest caliber; those with the character and personality as well as the intellect and knowledge necessary for the discharge of high office. Thereafter, they must be given responsibility from the very start; the chance to succeed or fail. They must be given, during the early years, a wide experience of the business of government, of the various departments of state, of the different tasks involved: working out plans, controlling men, negotiating with other people or organizations, allocating budget money and so on. Since these problems are common to all departments, they can become familiar with the whole machine and their superiors can discover in which particular areas their greatest talents lie. As they progress, they must be given wider and wider responsibilities, an increasing measure of independence, greater projects to bring to a successful conclusion. Having shown themselves outstanding in all these matters, they can then be invited to attend and contribute to discussions of high policy. And if in this final test of quality they show wisdom and a firm grasp of the most important affairs, they are adjudged fit to be numbered among those, the Cabinet who guide the whole enterprise. This would seem to be ideal.

But what actually happens? And at the very outset, the choice is restricted to MPs of the party in power; probably four hundred persons, including a sprinkling of the very young, the very old, the very forward, the very backward and the plain ordinary. Even the way these four hundred have been selected is a sorry farce. It is done by the committees of the constituency parties. "Arrogant women in funny hats for the Conservatives, disgruntled men in grubby macs for the Socialists," as an irate Minister once said. No one knows what on earth these committees are actually looking for, but it is quite clear that only by the purest chance can they choose someone capable of government. Only those who understand what governing demands, usually only those who have themselves successfully governed, can choose others to perform the same function. No one would ask the Mothers Union, for instance, to select the top management of Courtaulds. But this is how, in effect, the top management of the country is selected, since it is only for those candidates who please these absurd committees that the electorate is allowed to vote.

Pity the poor candidate. If his selection is a farce, his training is a travesty. He wins his election; his party is put in power. If he is one of the sixty chosen immediately for office, he will be pitchforked straight into a ministry. If he is not, he becomes a backbencher, where he will have no chance whatever to lay so much as a fingertip on the process of government, let alone get to grips with it. He controls nothing, arranges nothing, orders nothing. Nor can he learn by observing others how to do these things, since the process of government is not carried out in the House of Commons but in the Ministries of Whitehall. And he is certainly not welcome there, even as an eager-eyed apprentice. The most he can hope for is that he will be selected for one of the many all-party delegations which go off on nice free trips abroad to watch the process of government in newly-independent countries. He is moreover all the time aware that at any moment, and at the latest in five years, he might be chucked out of Parliament altogether and have to go back to work. Prudence therefore insists that, while striving to attract the notice and favor of his new masters and learn their ways, he must also retain the approval of his old. Indeed, if he is wise, he will try to keep working at his old job. If nothing else, it will give him something productive to do while he is a member of parliament.

And suppose the day finally comes when, though completely untutored, he has a deserved success and is given a ministry. Suppose he is made Minister of Health. This is a stupendous managerial job. He would be responsible for hundreds of hospitals, thousands of clinics, tens of thousands of doctors and nurses, a vast and grasping drug industry, a vital research program. In short, the health of a nation. With a press that personalizes everything, he would find within a week that he was apparently only the begetter of far-reaching plans begun three years previously. "Smith Acts on Hospitals," "Smith's Blueprint for Tomorrow" and all the rest of it. After a fortnight he would find himself responsible for mistakes made ages before by others. After a month he might start to believe it.

Assuming he managed to resist these blandishments,

and still realized that he knew about as much as the man in the street about it, he set out to discover how the system works. Even the most brilliant manager would need at least a year with no distractions to find out how the ministry ticks; to discover its weaknesses and its strengths and to plan its future. The task set him would be extraordinarily difficult even in the best conditions. But he would have the worst conditions!

He would have to nurse his constituency, attend party meetings, take part in television programs, talk to journalists, report to Buckingham Palace, turn up at public dinners, receive deputations of doctors, nurses, patients, radiologists, chemists, drug manufacturers, equipment makers, anti-abortionists, and fluoridation fanatics. He would have to formally open hospitals, research laboratories, X-ray centers, nursing colleges, and sewage farms. He would attend meetings of Government committees and Cabinet committees; Parliamentary debates and questions. And if, for lack of any of these things to do, he *did* manage occasionally to get down to work in his office, every time a certain bell rang he would have to hustle out and go across to Parliament to cast his vote on some vital medical issue like the nationalization of steel in order to help save the whole government from being thrown out.

It is plain that this system could only have been designed in order to make it very difficult for him to govern. What makes it *impossible* for him to govern is someone at his Ministry called the Permanent Secretary. The Permanent Secretary will listen attentively and respectfully to all the new Minister's suggestions and theories, then he will demonstrate that all those of which he and his staff disapprove are impossible in practice. Yes, we tried putting the drugs contract up for bid, but all the bids were about the same. Yes, that was suggested four years ago but the Hospital Workers Union refused to co-operate. Yes, we'd like to integrate the clinics with the hospitals, but the Local Authorities refuse and we have no powers of coercion. Yes, house physicians should be paid more but the Treasury won't release the money. Yes, we did a contingency study for modernizing Mental Hospitals in 1960, and the minimum cost was £260 million—and that was at 1960 prices. What—you want to abolish the prescription charge? Oh well, that knocks out all the other schemes forever. It was the only fund for raising doctors and nurses pay, modernizing the pre-1900 hospitals. . . .

The new Minister, hopelessly at sea, will find that the Permanent Secretary has everything at his fingertips. All the facts and figures, the stumbling blocks, the precedents, the past experience, the practicalities. He knows all the right people and all the right dodges. He alone knows what is desirable, what is possible, what is impossible, and what is unthinkable. And if the Minister, foolishly, tries to influence matters by going below the Permanent Secretary to the more junior officials he will find that, since he has no influence on their careers, no power of hire and fire, they have not the slightest interest in ingratiating themselves with him. In a year or two, he will be gone. The Permanent Secretary will not. It is not difficult to guess which damages a Civil Service career more—frustrating a Minister or irritating a Permanent Secretary. In short, the Minister finds that while he is, indeed, in office, he will never be in power.

He therefore leaves his ministry alone and concentrates on putting up a good show in Parliament. At least if he makes his mark there he can expect, if the worst comes to the worst and he is relieved of office, to be given a Life Peerage and some completely sinecure duty or other. His aim must be to keep up the most elaborate pretense of being pretentious and deceitful, in all of which he is given much assistance by the language of Parliament, which has been designed exactly for his predicament— that he must say one thing and mean either another or else nothing at all. Thus:

"My honorable and learned friend opposite" means "My disreputable and ignorant enemy."

"I shall require notice of that question"—"You're right."

"Let us not waste time scoring debating points"— "You're right."

"Under certain circumstances, given a favorable opportunity, I do not deny that such a course is, if not probable, at least not entirely out of the question"—"My God, you're right!"

"Perhaps the honorable member misunderstood me"— "I lied."

"I evidently misheard the honorable member"—"He lied."

"If the interests of this great nation require"—"I'm about to be fired."

"The interests of my constituents"—"I've *been* fired."

"This great party"—"I've been offered a Life Peerage."

Still, it is patently impossible for the United Kingdom to have no government at all. And it is obvious, when one looks at the situation carefully, to see who is doing the governing. It is the senior Civil Servants. They do indeed have the rigorous selection process, the probationary period, the apprenticeship, the wide experience of the different aspects of government, the ever-increasing responsibility and authority. They have the day to day contact with the practical realities of governing. They have the continuity, whatever "government" may be in office, whatever politician they are given as minister. They provide, say, Treasury policy as a single continuing thing, irrespective of which Government is in power. Even the Common Market decision is really a Civil Service decision. (And the French Civil Service at that.) They pretend they are merely high level clerks, "the administration," humbly and anonymously carrying out orders, executing other men's visions. It is true that they are anonymous. They do not have to answer to the public, or to government committees. They might even be humble. Nevertheless, they are our government. For the system, by its very nature, forces them to be the people who take the long-term decisions and formulate the advanced policies, even if the documents carry a politician's signature and the television screen carries a politician's smile.

The question that arises now is, if the Civil Servants are doing the governing, what are the politicians doing? Well, what is it that their habits seem to suggest? What use is there in their habit of mingling with all sorts and conditions of people; their habit of reading all manner of newspapers and periodicals; their habit of inviting their constituents to come to them and tell them their troubles; their habit of trying to detect and interpret even the slightest changes in the public mood and atmosphere and then trying to find "policies" that will appeal to and suit these changes? These, of course, are not the arts of government. But they *are* the arts of advertising and public relations. And that is what the politicians are doing. They are handling the PR and advertising for the true, concealed government of the Civil Servants.

If one equates government with management and politics with public relations, the parallels are obvious. Management and government are concerned with solving problems; PR and politics are concerned with shelving them. Management and government are about long-term realities; PR and politics are about short-term appearances. Management and government are about finding the right course of action; PR and politics are about finding the right form of words. Management and government are about precise instructions; PR and politics are about vague promises. Management and government are about steering a ship on a long, steady voyage; PR and politics are about surf-riding, catching the wave of public opinion with the plank of their "policy." Management and government are about making the right decisions; PR and politics are about making sure they cannot be proved to have made the wrong ones.

Once it is understood that politicians are public relations officers for their publicity-shy bosses, the Civil Service Permanent Secretaries, Parliament and politics become intelligible. Their power is the power of the PR man who decides the form and timing of announcements, who can sometimes influence events by saying to a firm that's in a bad way, "We cannot accept your account unless you change certain products or practices because we know— and we are experts in this—" Elected representatives are often very helpful to those who really govern. Their function is to conduct the government's "Can you tell margarine from butter?" campaigns, to judge what will please people and what will not; what is possible in terms of public opinion. But the Civil Servants are the judges of what is possible in terms of the realities of the business; what the doctors can be fobbed off with, how much America can be persuaded to fork over, how much unemployment the economy can stand, how many miles of new road can be built, how many miles of old railway torn up and so on. That was what was so ridiculous about the Conservative Party's hiring Colman, Brentis, and Varley. It was like J. Walter Thompson's hiring Doyle, Dane, Bernbach.

The only thing wrong with the situation, apart from the fact that it conceals the way the English are really governed, is that it needs pulling together at the very top. England needs, above the two groups, people who have the advantages of both and the disadvantages of neither. People with the permanence of Civil Servants and yet the public-opinion sensitivity of politicians. Not anonymous people, but people well and widely known and respected; not tarred with the brush of either party, yet able to move freely among the supporters of both parties. People who will be trusted and respected by ambassadors and dustmen and generals and bishops and criminals and High Commissioners and Permanent Secretaries and old men and housewives and party leaders.

Well, not people. Because a group of people could never achieve this miracle. But one person could. That is what the extraordinary English system of government needs. One person to hold it together. And, of course, that is what the extraordinary English system of government has got.

All we need to do is to restore the monarchy to its position under Elizabeth I, before it started to go wrong, and then, while Sir Walter Heath and Sir Francis Wilson do their splendid publicity stunts with cloaks and bows and tobacco and so on, the business of the Queen's Government can be carried on firmly and successfully for the first time in three and a half centuries. God Save the Queen!

14

Politics and Money

ONE confusing aspect of English politics remains to be cleared up: it is the ceremony known as a General Election. We know that elections can have nothing to do with government, because Civil Servants are not elected. They are selected. Elections have nothing to do with politics, either. The English do not, contrary to what politicians and foreigners imagine, walk down their High Street after a general election murmuring to themselves, "Whoopee, I'm in Harold Wilson's new society now." They do not call over the back garden fence to their neighbors, "I say, this is a bit different from the old Alec Douglas-Home days, isn't it?" And they do not, as they clock in at work, cry out, "I'm going forward with Labor this morning."

Life does change, even in England, but it changes gradually and in ways that pay no heed to politicians. Frozen vegetables and broiler chickens have probably had a much more profound effect on English lives than all the post-war Cabinet ministers put together. The event for which many people will best remember Harold Wilson's famous 100 days is the appearance everywhere of the fibretip pen. That really *was* a change. And England's victory in the World Cup had a greater influence on us all than Labor's victory in the general election.

Much of the misunderstanding is due to the fact that political journalists report general elections and political scientists comment on them. But this is only because a newspaper's basic idea is that today is different from yesterday; if it isn't, they have to create the illusion that it is. They have to pretend that things like the country's defense policy and financial policy and educational policy are going to change dramatically if one set of politicians rather than another is elected. But two minutes' reflection on the facts of daily life are enough to convince one that this is a fairy tale believed in only by politicians and journalists. Mind you, fifty million people do not go through all the convulsions and excitements of an election for no reason at all. The English aren't mad. They are not prepared to waste their time and energy on purposeless nonsense. There is a clue to what lies behind it all in this report in the *Sunday Mirror:* "The Pigalle night club will be doing its bit for politics on the night of the General Election. The line of chorus girls will be clad exclusively in blue, red, and yellow rosettes. Every time the Tories, Socialists, or Liberals lose a seat, off will come the appropriate rosette."

Now what is that reminiscent of? Specially chosen maidens. The most beautiful, but untouchable. Virtuous and pure, yet, as the night wears on, both responding to and provoking the mounting passion and excitement by divesting themselves of the symbolic silks which protect their chaste bodies from the worshipping multitude. And then the climax. The last rosette is plucked and tossed aside. The maidenly flesh is ravished and consumed (only symbolically, of course; the English are not given to filthy orgies) and the multitude, in the same moment exhausted and refreshed, can go about their business as far, far better people than they were before.

If that sounds like some primitive religious festival, it is because an English election *is* a primitive religious festival.

The pre-election period, when many of the enjoyable programs disappear from television screens and are replaced by the hideous boredom of election broadcasts, has its counterpart in most religions. It is the tribal ritual of self-denial and purification, expunging the self-indulgent sins of the rest of the year by asceticism and renunciation. Christians call it Lent, Jews call it Passover; Muslims call it Ramadan. And at the end of this prolonged fast, all religions have a feast. Easter for Christians, the last day of Passover for Jews, Al Fitr for Muslims, and so on. For the English, it is General Election Nights, when all the ghastly, mortifying broadcasts and speeches are over, and the people stay up late eating and drinking and exulting in the downfall of those who had previously set themselves up as mighty men.

An anthropologist would point out, too, that many

religions have a sort of mock-king, a joke-hero, chosen by the tribe to be fêted for a brief while and then destroyed. Feste, in Twelfth Night, represents the medieval English "Lord of Misrule" who was descended from one of these figures. Macaulay has described "The priest who slew the slayer and shall himself be slain," the Roman figure, often a slave, who lived in a sacred grove; he became the priest-king by killing the previous one, and the next one had to kill him. A similar ceremony occurred in the Eleusinian mysteries at Athens, re-created in *The King Must Die*. The idea was widespread throughout the ancient world. It is an atonement ritual. The wrath of the natural elements is personalized into the wrath of certain gods. And once the rain and the wind and fire and earthquake and sun and sea become mighty persons, they can be propitiated. Hence the idea of making sacrifices to them. Then comes the notion that great events need even greater offerings, and thus the sacrifice of noblemen or kings, as with Iphigenia and Isaac. Understandably, this gets pretty unpopular with noblemen and kings, so they cook up the idea of the mock-king; the king for a day who is made great in order to be a worthy sacrifice. And this is what happens in British elections. Once they are seen as a national ritual of atonement, everything falls into place.

For example, the pundits and political scientists are all very concerned about the way we are moving towards "presidential government." They say we ought to be concerned with policies and parties and not with the personality of any one man. Nevertheless, we continue to see the election as Wilson versus Heath. And this is because the English want a single joke-king, a genuine human sacrifice, not abstract ideas or anonymous groups. The function of the joke-king is that of scapegoat: all the sins of the tribe will be heaped on him. So the election is to decide who shall be that ritual scapegoat for a period of anything up to five years. It enables the English to pretend that their own faults are, in fact, the faults of this figure, so whatever goes wrong in that period—through bad industrial management, or timid civil servants, or stupid generals, or inept local councils—can all be blamed on him.

The two or more figures who vie for the post of joke-king have to try to guess where the community's deepest feelings of guilt lie and promise to atone for them. Sometimes the English feel most guilty about their callousness toward older members of the tribe, and so "Increased pensions" is a good scapecry. Sometimes it is the ignorance and willfulness of our children, and then the slogan is "Education." Sometimes it is inefficiency at work, and then it is "Modernization." Sometimes it is laziness, so the aspiring joke-king calls for "Shoulders to the wheel." Each joke figure has a chance to guess which part of their behavior the English feel worst about, and the one who guesses right is the one who is chosen.

The period of electioneering is the time when the potential scapegoats offer themselves to the people and submit themselves to various tests, more or less barbarous, to prove their worth. Time and custom have established various ways of doing this. There is the taunting, in which an aspiring joke-king used to be pricked and prodded by healthy young noblemen with the object of making him wince with pain. The joke-king has to show a certain toughness and durability or the gods will not accept him as a worthy sacrifice. The English call this taunting process an "impartial television interview." Each aspirant has to submit, before the whole population, or such of it as is interested in this part of the festival, to insolent, needling questions and brutal gibes. The joke-king must appear to treat all the questions seriously. Although he need not necessarily answer them properly he must never be at a loss for one or other of several invocations which are laid down in the election ritual.

The first is the proper response to a very, very sharp question that really pierces to the heart of things. He must be able to *destroy* the question—"That question is based on a confusion of thought. Really, there are two distinct and separate matters here. The first one is. . . ." He then picks a question he would like to answer. Or: "Just tell me young man, have you ever had to negotiate on behalf of two million people? You haven't. Well, let me tell you. . . ." It can also be done more indirectly: "That is a very good question and I would like to thank you for asking it. Let me answer it by asking you one. . . ." The joke-king must demonstrate that he is able to get over the shock of a sharp question without flinching and, further, turn it into a question that causes him no pain.

He must be able to *unload the question*. If it contains

any assertion or assumption, he must realize that he is supposed to forget the question and query the assumption. If the taunter says: "A lot of people have suggested you made a mistake in . . ." the correct response is: "Who has suggested this? Who are these people? Name me twelve of them." The taunter will then pass on to something else.

He must be able to *make it all appear an act.* "You know, I've come to the conclusion that I don't agree with what you suggested I should answer to that question when we were talking about this earlier. The *real* answer is. . . ." Thus, just for a moment, he puts the taunter in place of himself as aspiring joke-king and then speedily knocks him down.

He must be able to *use the time factor.* He must say, "That is a very interesting question and there are nine points I would like to make in answer to it." There is never time for nine points. So the taunter will have to say: "Perhaps you can make the three most important ones?" and the way is then open for the joke-king to say with utmost solemnity "No it's far too important a question to answer superficially. If I can't answer it fully, I'd rather not answer it at all."

He must be able to *invoke the plea of secrecy.* "There's a very good and full answer to that question, but it is involved with some things that are being confidentially discussed at this very moment. I'm afraid that's something I really *can't* talk about for another week or two."

The last of the stock invocations he must be able to

[187]

seek refuge in is *long, pointless narrative.* "Well, when I first entered public life, a good many years ago, more years in fact than I like to remember, my wife said to me, well, she wasn't my wife then as a matter of fact. My word, no. It *was* a long time ago. We had both just been elected to the Worplesden Urban District Council. Well, oddly enough, the same sort of thing that you are asking about arose then. In a minor way, of course. But the principle was the same. Principles always are you know, and I'm glad to say I haven't changed mine. Nor has my wife. At all events. . . ." This secondary use of the *time factor* will, if he is a worthy joke-king, enable him to connect the end of his rambling story in some way with the question.

After the taunting, there is the clowning. In this, the joke-king has to go through a perfectly serious and solemn solo performance on television to show that he can sound and look like a genuine king. He has to use certain ritual phrases like "England expects. . . . There's a difficult time ahead. . . . The Dunkirk spirit. . . . Forward into Europe" and use magic signs called graphs and pretend, perfectly straight-faced, that he can expound complicated fiscal and economic problems in five minutes. And all the time he is doing this, the people sit at home laughing at him and making rude signs and interpolating ribald remarks. He, knowing this is going on in millions of homes, has nevertheless to remain serious. All this is an electronic development in the days when aspiring joke-kings are given exactly the same set of facts, and nowadays exactly the same television

[188]

film scenes, and each one has to use them the best way he can to divine the tribal guilt feelings and prove himself the best choice for their propitiation. The facts and the film are about children in playgrounds, nurses in hospitals, smoking factory chimneys, and houses without lavatories.

The reigning joke-king has to say: "Our children have never been stronger. . . . We have never been healthier. . . . We have never been richer. . . . We have never had fewer slums."

The one who wants to topple him has to say: "Our children have nothing to do but play because there are not enough classrooms for them. . . . Our nurses will go on strike unless we pay them more, and then there will be nobody to soothe us when we are ill. . . . All this smoke is making everything dirty and giving us cancer. . . . I will give each family a nice house of their very own."

The people then make up their minds about how naughty they have been. If they think they have been well-behaved under the reigning joke-king, they choose him again. If they think they have been very sinful, they choose one of his rivals. If it is raining, they don't care much either way, taking the view that if the aspiring joke-kings can't choose a fine day between them they really *are* buffoons. They are much more concerned by this time with the forthcoming feast of the results in which, as the elected joke-king and his elected retinue of joke-wizards and tumblers and jugglers make mock-threats and promises of the use they will make of the "power" they have been given,

[189]

the celebrations reach a climax. The conquering joke-king
is driven to Buckingham Palace, where he kisses the hand
of a real monarch.

This signals the end of the festival and immediately
the taunting and mockery stops. From now on the joke-king
is treated just as if he were a real king. He is allowed to
appoint some of his friends as joke-courtiers, each owing
special allegiance to him and each serving a particular god,
like money, or war, or plague, and each with his own place
of worship and his own ritual chariot (black Humbers,
chosen to look a bit like the Daimlers and Cadillacs that
real monarchs use, but not *too* like them). They are given
big empty rooms to sit in, and the real rulers, the civil
servants, have to pretend to consult them on all important
matters of state business and pretend that their orders come
from the joke-king and his courtiers.

If a joke-courtier proves incapable of pacifying the
particular god he is supposed to be serving, then he is
ritually sacrificed and another put in his place. If all the
gods are angry together, then the Great God himself becomes wrathful and all the joke-courtiers and the joke-king
himself are offered up in one great ritual sacrifice call The
Fall of the Government.

The name of the Great God is Democracy. His worship is the official state religion. Our actual rulers do not
believe in him but they encourage us to do so by giving
us what they assure us are magic tokens called votes.

Of course, it is very expensive to maintain a Great

God, real rulers, and all the court of the joke-king. Therefore our rulers have invented a special form of joke-money
with which to pay for all this. It is called Public Money,
but it is quite different from the public's money.

The public's money takes two forms, pocket money
and check money. Pocket money is the real thing. It is still
a pleasure to have in your hand. As somebody wrote in the
Daily Express: "Instead of us switching to decimal coinage,
why don't the foreigners change to sterling?" It has a nice feel
to it. It is heavy or crisp. It clinks or rustles. Receiving it
causes pleasure. Parting with it causes pain. It is the stuff
you get at the end of a hard week's work; the stuff for
which you surrender yourself and submit to the authority
and discipline of other people. It disappears across shop
counters and bars. It goes pretty well as fast as it comes.
As a young builder's laborer told the West London magistrate: "I make about twenty-eight quid a week. I pay three
pounds ten for my lodgings and send four pounds to my
mum and I enjoy myself with the rest of it. I'm a member
of six strip clubs in the West End. That runs away with
most of it." Pocket money makes a nice bulge in your wallet
and it stacks up well on the mantelpiece. You can keep it
in a sock or under your pillow, or wherever you like. Best
of all, you know it is all yours.

Check money is not quite so real as pocket money.
Paying out by check does not hurt anything like as much as
paying out of pocket money, and there is always the curious
feeling that you're better off with a fifty pound roll in your

pocket than with a two hundred pound deposit in the bank. The unreality of check money and the unreal way it is dealt with can be demonstrated by going into a shop, buying something that costs about ten pounds and then writing out a check for it. Unless the shopkeeper knows you, he will ask you to write your address on the back—on the strange theory that you might forge a name but never an address. That you might sign "The Duke of Norfolk" on the front but that you would always put "Three, Railway Cuttings" on the back. Although it is genuine public's money, check money is never quite as welcome as the pocket sort, though, on the other hand, the penalties for default are less arduous. If you default on pocket money, the bailiffs come in and take away the furniture, perhaps even evict you from the house.

But if you default on check book money, the worst that usually happens is expulsion from the check book class. Fortnum's or Claridge's or Rolls Royce or White's or Harrods aren't going to sue for a few hundred pounds. You may be expelled from the club, blacklisted, refused an account, but that is all. For all that it is slightly flamboyant, check money is still related to work and sweat. The pay-slip and the bank statement are an expression of hours put in, meetings attended, fish caught, gutted, and sold.

But when you move into the realm of the money used by our rulers, when you take a look at Public Money, you discover that it has nothing at all in common with the public's money. Public Money has no connection with the real world of work and toil and getting tipsy. The Treasury talks about an annual revenue of thousands of millions of pounds, but nothing is manufactured or sold in Whitehall. Nor, on the whole, does anyone sweat. Public Money represents no reward for someone's labor; it just flutters down like snowflakes. Civil servants—who run their private lives, like everyone else, on pocket money and check money —regard Public Money and the collection of it as a game of Monopoly, in which a huge mountain of so-called pounds is left to them alone to deal with because nobody else knows how to play. And members of the general public, who are supposed to contribute this money, feel just the same as the civil servants about it, because half the time, by a diabolical plan, they do not notice that they have contributed it. No one stands at the shop door to collect purchase tax and we forget exactly how much gasoline costs the gas companies to produce. In any case, even when we remember what we have contributed and try to find out where it has gone, we lose sight of it in the vast, jolly pile of Monopoly money with which we are confronted. That thousand million pounds for a new airplane, thinks the ordinary Englishman, cannot possibly have anything to do with the fact that I ran out of money for cigarettes last week.

But Public Money never runs out. If Whitehall has not got enough it simply asks for more. Lots of their projects get into what would be called debt if they were dealing in pocket money or check money, but with Public Money there is no such thing as debt. Only miscalculation, or under-estimating. And whereas the penalty for miscalculating pocket or check money can range from poverty to imprisonment, the penalty for miscalculating Public Money is a transfer to another department with a trifle less Public Money to play with. The worst that can happen is that the expected C.B.E. in the New Year's Honors List will be delayed for twelve months, or commuted to an O.B.E.

The great job of spending Public Money is that no one but Civil Servants can comprehend the sums they deal with. No member of the public can talk meaningfully about £100,000,000. But a committee of Civil Servants can slice that sort of sum up, double it, count it as below the line expenditure, get it from the Bank of England, spend it all on some system for stamping little lions on eggs and regard it as a good morning's work. They will then turn their attention to someone like Pauline Gough, who set the Ministry of Education a severe Public Money problem a few years ago. She lived five and a half miles from school. So did Sheila Gough, naturally enough since she was Pauline's sister, and the lived in the same house. The rules for dispensing Public Money sanctioned the hire of a taxi to take Sheila to school in the morning and bring her home in the evening, because there was no bus and she was only seven years old. But they would not and did not permit the trifling additional cost entailed if Pauline rode in the back seat with her sister. She had to walk. Because she was eight. The sum of money involved was eleven shillings a day. And it was argued about for weeks. It was the sort of money everyone can understand, but £2,000,000,000 for defense! What on earth does it *mean*? Nobody actually misses that sort of Public Money; nobody feels it disappearing from his wallet. So nobody really cares about it.

And yet somebody benefits by dealing in these impossible sums of Public Money. Not by feathering their own nests, exactly, for the Civil Service operates with scrupulous personal honesty. And, of course, government is a nonprofit making business in the old-fashioned capitalist sense. But we have moved out of the old-fashioned capitalist era and into the new managerial era, and while there may be no capitalists in the Civil Service, there is a small army of managers.

Pleasure, for a manager, consists in retaining all the agreeable tasks and status-increasing apparatus of his office and delegating all the disagreeable bits to others. It lies in a higher rank, another personal assistant, suave luncheons with flattering tycoons who want Public Money for one of their projects, increasing platoons of deferential subordinates. It lies, in short, in empire-building. And so the constant pressure within the Civil Service is for more and more sections, more and more departments, more ministries even, which have the additional merit of keeping Parliament and politicians sweet.

Whitehall never says, "What do we need and how shall we raise it?" It says, "How much can we raise and what shall we do with it?" For what it is after, like everyone else, is growth. And a study of the staff, expenditure and wages bill of the Civil Service shows it is one of our major growth industries. In July, 1964, Parliament ordained the amalgamation into one Ministry of the departments separately responsible for the armed forces, the navy, the army and the air force. Obviously, there would have been massive savings of money and staff if the Ministry of Defense treated the three services simply as different units of the same service. Massive savings of managers, too, including generals and admirals and air marshals. In fact, the Whitehall service staffs are larger than ever and the only real change is that there is now a mass of new "liaison" posts to help the integration! And this despite the strong desire of both Conservatives and Socialist politicians to cut the defense bill by streamlining the Services.

The English are always complaining about government waste and extravagance, but in the conventional sense the Civil Service is not at all bountiful, as anyone who visits a government office soon realizes. The cheapest and most uncomfortable furniture and decorations, the most disgusting canteens, waiting rooms so bleak that one is cringing with misery. No National Assistance widow is ever given an extra shilling to buy an extra cup of tea and a bun, no disabled pensioner in the outpatients' waiting room is ever provided with an armchair. In all these ways, there is no waste. But unnecessary departments, under-secretaries who need only be controllers, controllers who ought to be no more than principals, three sections responsible for what one could manage, projects focused, not on national need but on ministerial desire—that is another matter. It is "growth."

One ministry gave one of its Civil Servants the specific task of cutting down on over-staffing and empire-building. He guaranteed to do the job and then added, "But for a start I'll need another office, three assistants and fourteen secretaries."

15

Is England in Europe?

WHATEVER form our government has taken over the centuries—whether we were ruled by a monarch, or by nobles, or by Parliament, or by the civil service—in one aim it has been consistent: Keep away from Europe and keep Europe away. The simple and generally effective policy of England has been to encourage the Continentals to bash each other up and leave us alone. Only when one country started to get too good at bashing the other did we think it necessary to concern ourselves with Europe, and the great heroes of modern England—Marlborough, Wellington, Nelson, Kitchener, Montgomery, Lloyd George, Churchill—are the people who have stepped in to put uppity Continentals firmly in their place. Of course, we have always acted in accordance with the highest principles. We have never actually said we were trying to keep Europe divided and impotent. We have been upholding at various times international legality, self-determination, justice, freedom, democracy and the general right of foreigners to kick each other in the teeth. Humbug or not, the effect has been that England has not been successfully invaded by an army from the Continent since 1066.

It seems impossible that a policy that has succeeded so well for nearly a thousand years should ever be questioned. And yet for the past few years the English have found themselves debating, apparently quite seriously, whether or not they should join the European Economic Community, the Common Market. Has the millennium of division really come to an end? Certainly it seemed impossible to the Foreign Office even ten years ago when the Common Market was first formed and we were pressed to join by the French and Germans—indeed the whole six. However, this change, which was foreseen in the thirties and was blindingly obvious at the end of World War II, finally dawned on the Foreign Office about 1960 or 1961. Wars (especially after the atom bomb) were going to be economic and not military, and the largest economic groupings were going to do best in that kind of warfare. The Americans were a big group, the Russians were a big group, and quite clearly Europe had to be a big group, too, or else the separate countries had to throw in their lot with one or the other of the two existing big groups. Not surprisingly, a lot of Europeans decided to be a big group on their own.

This, of course, changed the situation of 500 years'

standing. From then on, keeping Europe divided did not create a balance of power, but a balance of impotence. The balance of power was to be served by Britain's throwing her weight into the third force, to create a unit of equal strength to the USSR and the USA. But the 500-year tradition of keeping out of European entanglements was too much for the Foreign Office to defy at that stage, and the Six started without us. The result was the one thing that Britain had schemed to avert for 500 years: a united Europe. The European Free Trade Association, the attempt to keep Europe economically divided, was the last feeble spasm of an exhausted political philosophy. The debate has taken in any number of points—effect on the Commonwealth, our special relationship with America, the role of sterling as a reserve currency, balance of trade, industrial competition, movement of labor, the price of food, and the demeanor of General de Gaulle, or Louis XIX, as he is known. Millions of words have been spoken and written about these impediments to our joining the Common Market; none at all about an obstacle more overwhelming than any of them. The blunt fact that the English don't like foreigners.

There have been many attempts to describe hell, but for Englishmen the best definition is that it is a place where the Germans are the police, the Swedish are the comedians, the Italians are the defense force, Frenchmen dig the roads, Belgians are the pop singers, the Spanish run the railways, the Turks cook the food, the Irish are the waiters, the Greeks run the government, and the common language is Dutch. Not that this is based on any real knowledge of foreigners. Far from it. Ask any average group of Englishmen what are the main products of our possible future colleagues and the consensus will be that the Spanish have something to do with making onions and omelettes; the Swiss, rolls; the Portuguese, men of war; the Italians, straw hats; the Dutch, auctions and courage; the French, dressing; and the Germans, measles. Foreigners are just not good enough for us, although we appreciate, of course, that it's not their fault. As Conservative politician John Hay told a questioner who referred to "Eyeties" and "Froggies" during a public meeting to discuss the Common Market at Sonning Common, in deepest Berkshire: "We as a nation must not sneer at others who perhaps have not had the same chances as ourselves." Perhaps that is why the immediate reaction of an Englishman confronted with a European who does not understand him is to speak very slowly and shout very loud, exactly the way one deals with the infantile and the senile.

The feeling that we are by nature superior to Europeans has been implicit in all our negotiations and discussions about the Common Market. No English politician or journalist or opinion-former of any kind has talked about joining Europe as if it were nice. They say it will be industrially beneficial, the saving of our run-down and incompetitive industries, a move in keeping with the times and all that sort of worthy stuff. Even its most ardent supporters never stand up and say it's simply a marvelous idea! That these closer links with Europeans are going to be stimulating and great fun and a source of enrichment to our lives. Because nobody in England would believe them. So far as we are concerned the only thing stimulating about Europe is the cheap liquor.

Our education has taught us that Europe is composed of knaves and fools who have spent most of recorded history retreating in disarray before our army and navy. There are exceptions, naturally. Maurice Chevalier is not a bad chap and Inspector Maigret seems a straightforward enough fellow. But on the whole Europeans are politically unstable, prone to fascism and communism and several governments a month. They either treated their royal families with brutal offensiveness or, if they still have the grace to support royal families, make them ride around on bicycles and send their children to council schools.

Is it then surprising that the English attitude toward the Common Market is that it is a painful, unpleasant, and humiliating thing that, even for the sake of economic salvation, is barely worth considering? Maybe it is calling the New World into existence to redress our bank balance in the old, but it is none the less unwelcome for that. Some idealists hoped that by encouraging us to have holidays abroad they would increase our liking for the continent and its occupants. On the contrary, it confirmed our dislike. The suggestion that these people have somehow found the secrets of commercial success and industrial

[203]

growth which have eluded decent English people is, quite frankly, not to be believed. Just look at the place. They drive on the wrong side of the road; their money is made of some tatty, tinny stuff or dirty bits of paper worth three-pence; they use illogical weights and measures, they fuss over their children and each other in exactly the sort of way one suspected of a continent which produced people like Freud with his nasty ideas; they gabble and wave their arms about as if they were all actors or something; they don't feed their cats and they don't train their dogs, but their goats, on the other hand, they seem to adore; every single one of them is out to take the maximum cash off English tourists while giving them minimum value, and they walk around as if they owned the place.

The extraordinary thing is that they do not even seem to see what they are missing by not being English themselves. They just carry on eating their extraordinary food-stuffs, talking their outlandish languages, making their sexy films and being rude to the English, all the while their breath smelling of garlic.

It is a reflection of the genial tolerance and innate good sense of the English that, in spite of all these acknowledged faults on the part of the Europeans, we were still prepared to deign to join their squalid little club. But an incredible thing happened. They didn't want us! Perhaps it is not really so incredible after all. We have always known what an ungrateful lot foreigners are however good we are to them. General de Gaulle himself would probably still be a Colonel if we had not let him take refuge over here in 1940, yet he seems to be the most ungrateful devil of the whole lot. Not only ungrateful, deceitful too. They go on pretending that the English might be a liability to Europe; pretending that they want to be a really unified group. It is quite incomprehensible that they should go on talking about us as a backward, fuddy-duddy, uncompetitive nation that tries to combine an attitude towards America of political servitude with one of moral superiority; and that is concerned exclusively with national advantage at everyone else's expense.

Of course the English would not object to being part of a wider, unified Europe, but is it not as plain as the nose on anyone's face, even a foreigner's, that the English would inevitably be at the top of that group? That's natural enough and obvious enough, surely? Not exactly leading. The English do not suggest *that*, because leading implies that the group is going somewhere, positively and purposefully. Not leading but *presiding*. The English accept the thought that the group should be bound together with noble resolutions, but obviously no nation, least of all the English, should have to change its ways to suit anyone else. The group should not actually do anything, or mean anything. We understand perfectly that it is necessary for the leaders of the Common Market countries to talk about a Europe in which being a European will in time come to mean more than being French or Dutch or German and so on, but isn't it a little bit absurd to try to pretend that it, or anything else, can ever come to mean more than being English? On that point we are bound to refer the so-called Europeans to a thousand years of history which no Treaty of Rome, however well-intentioned, can alter. Surely they must have noticed that the word "European," when spoken by an Englishman, does not include the English?

The Europeans have got to realize that they have a lot of soundly-based English distrust about foreigners to overcome. An opinion poll in London recently put the question: "Do you think Britain would do better to join Europe, or to strengthen the Commonwealth, or to concentrate on the special relationship with America?" Ninety-nine percent said "No."

In fact, the perfect solution to all this Common Market, European, third force, balance of power nonsense is lying to hand. The Europeans should join the Commonwealth. They would have many of the advantages, at present completely denied them, of being nearly English; they could be part of a trade association, which is the sort of thing they seem to enjoy; they would have access to a superb bureaucracy in Whitehall; and they could put forward nominees for the orders of chivalry and the peerage. All this and the House of Lords! What more could they want?

16

The
Englishman
Abroad

AN Englishman's home is his castle, but he likes occasionally to confirm his belief that there's no place like home. Travel narrows the mind, as that excellent old English saying has it. In 1956, about one and a half million of the English made a tour of inspection abroad, known to them colloquially as "going on holiday." In 1966, stories about the extraordinary things that went on abroad having spread far and wide, about five million went to have a look. This prodigious increase is ascribed by the economists to increasing affluence, and by travel agents, airlines, and foreign travel bureaus to a strong desire among the English for sun, good food, relaxation and a total freedom from worry and responsibility.

But their preparations for departure are not entirely consistent with this; they hardly behave like people about to enjoy themselves. Baedeker and the Edwardians thought

[207]

that vital requirements for travel beyond England's shores were: "Aspirin and quinine for fever, formamint and potassium chlorate for sore throat, veramon and pyramidon for headaches, bismuth and magnesia for indigestion, bromural for insomnia, cascara and Epsom salts for constipation, ammonia for scorpion bites, zinc or starch dusting powder for chafed sores, charcoal tablets and a body belt for diarrhoea, antiseptic wool, carbolic acid, boracic powder, iodine and corrosive sublimate tablets and a clinical thermometer." This list the New Elizabethans have made more formidable with the addition of plastic containers of many shapes and sizes for spare gasoline and drinking water; cooking stoves; tea pots and kettles; iron pills; wads of maps; a movie camera; and a book of crossword puzzles. Is this the apparatus of the lotus eater? Or of the missionary explorer?

What with checking this paraphernalia, the departure is not exactly the happiest moment of the year, that heart-stopping moment at the airport of, "No, *you* had the passports. I only had the traveler's checks." (Even worse if the passport applications have been dealt with by the Foreign Office official who, noticing that one woman from Leicester had described herself, in the section for "special peculiarities," as having hair which extended well below her knees entered simply on her passport, "Hairy legs.")

Once they are under way, do the English relax?

"How much was the petrol? Twenty-four francs? They overcharged you. I knew they would."

[208]

"Look at that! They don't even bother to go behind the hedge!"

"Fruit and chocolate will do unless we can find a place where they don't cook in that oil."

"I'd rather sleep in the car again than stay in a hotel like that."

"Tell him we're English; just *tell* him we're English."

"But I distinctly told them we didn't want a bathroom with one of these . . . things."

No, they do not relax. There is a continuous process of worry and argument, a permanent atmosphere of rush and urgency, especially over the sacred and arduous ritual duty of photography, hard enough with stills, almost overwhelming if it is a movie camera. Day after day the inspection goes on, seeing the prescribed sights, taking the obligatory pictures, driving the necessary distances against the clock, and all with the added hazards of strange languages and strange currencies. Most English tourists spend the odd breaks they get from peering through the windshield by squinting through a viewfinder. Does all this sound like a carefree life in the sun, away from the troubles that press down during the other fifty weeks of the year? Of course it doesn't. And two minutes listening to an Englishman's description of his "holiday" will prove it. With what relish he will tell of gastric disorders, carsick children, insolent officials, bad roads, missed routes, flies, bedbugs, cockroaches, noisy hotels, overcharging, swindling, and robbery, weak tea, gassy beer, stupid peasants, messed-about food, inadequate breakfasts, crowded coaches, bursting bladders, young children who lose their sandals, older ones who lose their virginity, sunburn, sea-sickness, and athlete's foot.

That is just for a start. After two minutes you will hear even more lurid details of the narrative. But however long you listen, and whichever variety of hardship befell the travelers you talk to, one single thread binds them all. They will all tell you they had a marvelous holiday.

Where is the connection? What can conceivably relate the relaxed sunbathing ideal of the brochure to the acute and protracted misery of driving to Athens in an Austin Mini with two small children, of whom at least one is always threatening that if it can't get out and go to the bathroom in sixty seconds it will have to go to the bathroom without getting out? How can the vision of the lithe brown body slicing into deep blue water have any-thing to do with the embarrassing reality of the lobster-red, blistered, corpulent figure trying to hold up three towels at once so that the wife can get herself dressed out of sight of a mob of lascivious natives?

That is exactly it. The barbarity of it all was what made it so marvelous. To talk about.

"Forty minutes standing in line and when she got her ice cream it tasted of garlic."

" 'Call this a row boat?' I said. 'We've got better on the lake in the park.' And then his old tub sank . . ."

"So after the fourth night next door to this French

couple, we asked for another room, with thicker walls. . . ."

"Stranded between Rome and Ostia with the rain coming down in buckets and this fool policeman asks for the green card . . ."

"Goat's milk! Can you imagine? . . ."

"Well, of course, poor Mary didn't know she wasn't supposed to swallow it. I mean, who would have thought of doing *that* with a sleeping pill?"

"The only one for sixty people; no bolt on the door, naturally. . . ."

"Everywhere you turn there's someone standing with his hand out for money. . . ."

" 'If you're so bloody clever how come you lost the war?' I said. That shut him up. . . ." "They laughed the other side of their faces when we told them what they could do with it; luckily we had a tin of bully beef left, so we didn't go hungry. . . ." " 'I'm afraid not sir' he said, 'We expect our guests to take a bath before they come. . . .' " "Well, he *called* himself a doctor, but all I can say is she could have had an English doctor's license taken away for it. . . ." "And the smell! . . . And the food! . . . And the noise! . . . And the PEOPLE!"

The barbarity subdued and the difficulty overcome— *this* is what makes an Englishman's holiday abroad marvelous. Holidays abroad are for the looking forward to and the looking back on, not for the actual enjoying. Fun to prepare the plan-of-campaign for, and to tell everyone about afterwards but hell to participate in. And the bit of the movie the returned holidaymaker likes to show you most is the bit with the biggest disaster in it. "See. That's it. Stuck like that for seven hours in the blazing sun. Had to round up seventeen locals to pull us out. God how they sweated! Had to tip the lot, of course, so that shot the day's spending money. Nothing but the awful local sausage. That's Joan eating it. Made her sick all night."

In the 16th century he explored the Pacific; in the 17th he traded in India; colonized America in the 18th; civilized Africa in the 19th. In the 20th century, the only challenge left for an Englishman is the Continent. And he meets it, head up, eyes front, every summer. Then, like any war veteran, he spends the autumn and winter swapping gory anecdotes about it with his friends. Thank goodness! Returned holidaymakers will compete violently in mileage traveled, especially per day, remoteness and acute hardship of place reached, number of sights seen as validated by luggage labels, passport stampings, and car stickers, and in general, suffering.

If the Continent ever pulls its socks up, the English will stop going there and turn their attention to America, where there is also plenty of room for improvement. Only in the two or three weeks of holiday abroad can the modern Livingstone, or Cook, or Scott become a tough explorer and face the real hardship of an uncivilized, un-English world; only in those few days of the year can he cease to be the subordinate of a subordinate of a subordinate and become instead what his heritage of English blood insists he really is—leader and captain of a small expedition carrying out a tough assignment among upstart natives in hostile territory. It's hell, of course, but it is, let's face it, a man's life! No wonder the wife hates it.

Millions of the English, of course, simply refuse to waste time or money on foreigners. The Continent, irritating enough in time of war, they feel, is utterly devoid of attraction in time of peace, and should be left to its own absurd devices. And so, the vast majority of the English stay at home, thinking sweet thoughts about their own fair country.

Every Englishman is a countryman at heart. However many years he may have lived in the city, he does not believe he really belongs there. As he looks out the window of his apartment over the vast desert of brick and concrete, relieved by a single pollarded plane tree, he has in his mind a vivid picture of the day when he will live in a thatched cottage with roses around the porch and hollyhocks in the garden, and breathe in the fresh air of the unspoiled countryside, while listening for the first Percy Edwards of Spring. It is a long distance love affair. The farther away the countryside is, both in miles and time since he was last there, the more desirable it becomes.

Everything he sees about him panders to his romantic illusion. Television commercials picture a countryside where it is always a sunny summer afternoon, never a wet and windy morning. Whether the commodity is milk or corn flakes or candy or cigars or motor cars or beer, the countryside has something to add to it. It stands for freshness, for purity, for fun and games, for country lanes dotted with young couples on the verge, for rustic stiles more sinned against than sinning. Insurance companies have posters of country villages, suggesting something real in an artificial world, something enduring and unchanging in a world where everything else seems to be going rapidly downhill. Every Englishman feels all this deep in his heart and it is for this reason that every doctor and dentist has in his waiting room a copy of the magazine *Country Life;* descriptive of rural pleasures and retreats, it is the most powerful anodyne known to English pharmacology.

To the *Sunday Mirror,* the English countryside is a girl in a bikini stretched at provocative length in a field of golden daffodils; to *The People* it is the sensational and scandalous discovery of a coven of witches in the Chiltern Hills; to *The News of the World* it is an unhappy ending to a picnic when a thirty-five year old attractive red-headed widow hitchhiked a ride in a lane five miles outside Chichester from a forty-two year old thick-set truck driver, who was sentenced to six months. But to all of them, it is something worth fighting for, and an Englishman gets tremendously upset if he hears of anything that threatens to disturb or destroy his idyll. He has probably never seen the place and probably never expects to see it. His opposition is rooted more in Thoreau than in anger. He has his National Trust, his Men of the Trees society, and preservation councils for just about every hill and valley south of the Caledonian Canal, and any scheme for moving smoky power stations away from crowded cities and onto empty moors, any proposals for a satellite town which will relieve the squalor of urban slums, anything which might interfere with the vast tracts of land he calls his countryside, will meet with implacable, though fruitless, opposition.

The only schemes exempt from his wrath are those for building highways. And this is understandable, since it is only because of the highways and trunk roads and railways that he knows the countryside is there at all. If all the countryside were removed except for what is visible from the railways and main roads, ninety-nine per cent of the English would be none the wiser.

For it is only the *idea* of the countryside that the English are in love with. The reality they in fact detest. For the past two centuries the driving force of English society has been to get away from the country and into the towns and cities at the greatest possible speed and in the greatest possible numbers. Something like eighty per cent have achieved it, and the rest need hardly bother. Instead of rushing into town from the countryside, they find it easier to wait in the countryside for the towns to rush out to them, most English farmers having one field given over to wheat, one to potatoes and one to a housing estate. Indeed, last year Wembley Stadium was voted the best kept village in Middlesex.

Having got away from the country, the English have

created for themselves an environment as much unlike it as possible, and whenever they venture back into it, they find it almost unbearable. It is not just because of the crawly things and the horny things which menace them in ways undreamed of in their cities; it is also because of the total absence of anything to do. According to the television commercials the Englishman can go for leisurely walks with his girl friend through waist-high corn, he coveting her pack of cigarettes, she his box of milk chocolates. In practice, these and similar notions are neither forthcoming nor attractive when he actually gets to the country. There is nothing he can do there that he cannot do in the city, although it is true that with so much more space available he is rather less likely to get caught.

Above all, there is a very great deal of ghastly silence. The countryside is at best a lunch break on the way from the urban metropolis to a seaside one—which appeals in direct ratio to its similarity to the city just left. The traveler might drive a hundred yards off the main road for his picnic, but, finding even his transistor radio incapable of completely dispelling the eerie silence, he will soon be back on the strip of grass alongside the main road, where he and his family will be able to enjoy their meal, thanks to the comforting roar of the cars hurtling past at the rate of a thousand an hour. Many of these cars will be heading for one of the vast car parks, complete with cafeteria, amusement arcade, rest rooms, and souvenir shop, which cater to the Englishman's inability in any circumstances, including a visit to the country, to range more than two hundred yards in any direction from his car. He does not understand the complaint that these car parks are spoiling the countryside. Well sited at the top of various small rises, these are the only places, he will point out, from which he can see the countryside. The fact that there might actually be a real human being out there looking at his car park is so manifestly absurd and far-fetched as not even to enter his head. Safe and snug in his little bit of town slap in the middle of Dartmoor, his tiny *urbs in rure,* he gazes over the vast deserted panorama for a moment or two and then, reassured that nobody is mucking England about, gets in his car, heads for the nearest clover leaf junction and is quickly back in the mainstream of life.

To someone brought up with central heating, electricity, running water, regular buses and trains, taxis, good roads, a choice of shops, convenient schools, heaps of entertainment, and a different restaurant for every night of the month if he wants it, the country is not merely uncivilized. It is that by definition. It is ghastly! That sweet, unspoiled village of the posters and television commercials —every house is swept by hurricane drafts and riddled with creeping things; half the inhabitants have to draw their water from a well and three-quarters have outside privies. It is not much good having a house that is five minutes from the station if the station is now two hours walk from the next station. There is nothing to talk about and nowhere to go and nothing to do that doesn't get a city man into trouble. (England's urban court reports are full of strange goings-on, but none of them quite so incredibly strange as the goings-on dealt with by the rural magistrates.) Such beings, presumably human, as he might encounter wear huge boots and shapeless thorn-proof tweeds and they lean, wordlessly, on five-barred gates smoking meditative, stubby pipes. And that's only the women. The men shake their fists at him.

There is, about the countryside, something else that makes the average Englishman feel especially uncomfortable and guilty. It is the fact that it is full of delightful animals. The English love animals. That is a well-known fact. They have dogs and cats and parakeets and watch Zoo Time on television. Their childhood friends are Bugs Bunny and Mickey Mouse and Toad and Badger and all the rest of the nursery menagerie. But in the country, most of his old friends don't last any longer than it takes the farmer to load his .22 rifle. In 1940, when the English were alone and besieged by foreigners and food was very hard to come by, the song the whole nation sang with gusto was, "Run rabbit, run rabbit, run, run, run; Don't give the farmer his fun, fun, fun; We'll get by without our rabbit pie; So run rabbit, RUN, RUN, RUN!" But even as flop-eared bunny disappears safely down his burrow, the townsman knows that some other soft-eyed creature is making the last sacrifice. And making it for him! That's what worries him so. The whole place is a secret slaughter-house for those marvelous restaurants of his. The countryside has an unpleasant way of reminding him of what he would like to forget about every time he eats a tender veal cutlet: that little calf looking up at its mother with appealing brown eyes. Some callous country-man wrang the neck of his Christmas turkey. His bacon and sausage were once Little Pig Robinson. And Larry the Roast Lamb! It just doesn't bear thinking about.

No wonder the English keep as far away from the countryside as they possibly can. Their illusions and evasions could never survive contact with reality. But there is one beneficiary. And that is the English farmer. He is the man who long ago stopped keeping up with the Joneses and concentrated on keeping up with the Rothschilds.

To the townsman, the farmer is still Farmer Giles, a weather-beaten, bow-legged rustic with an ash stick and a funny accent, wading ankle-deep in the muck of his farmyard or gripping a pint of ale in his gnarled fist. "There's nothing like a good bit of dung," he says once in a while. But only for the sake of his public image; for he knows that all the time the townies are giggling and nudging each other over his charming earthiness, they will not bother to question why he should have subsidies, support and feather-bedding on a scale so large that nobody else would dare try and claim it, and pay wages on a scale so small that nobody else would dare try and get away with it. If they saw him driving to market in the Jaguar, or his wife parking the Bentley outside Harrods, they might stop and ask themselves what farming is really all about. And they would soon realize that when Farmer Giles talks about making a stack, he doesn't mean hay; and that if he wanted to mechanize his farm he would suggest to the Government that they go fifty-fifty—the taxpayer providing gas and oil and Farmer Giles the air and the water. But ask him about dangerous subjects like Europe and he will become sly, bucolic old Farmer Giles again and sound rather like the farmer in Bungay, Suffolk, who, when asked by the local paper what he thought about joining the Common Market, replied "I am damned if I am going to drive my pigs all the way to Brussels. . . ."

The listeners dissolve into laughter at his hopelessly uncommercial approach, but love him for his uncomplicated insularity. He knows he has to be that way, for the English love of his countryside is, first and foremost, a defiant assertion of Englishness. Townsmen will protest in their millions about desecrating the countryside with high tension towers, but the farmers never join in until they think they might not get enough compensation for the scrap of land they give up; only then do they become staunch preservationists of our rural heritage. The result of *their* communion with nature has been to make them the most avidly materialistic people in the land. Such time as they can spare from consultations with their accountants is spent in nagging the humble, underpaid scientists who, back in their smoky, noisy cities, do their best to meet the farmer's constant cry for more and more astounding chemicals to reduce his heavy burden of toil. What they want, ideally, is something which will encourage their hens to lay eggs so fast they just stand on tiptoe all day shouting "Catch!" and an injection for their beasts compounded of male hormones, female hormones and a tranquilizer so that bull and cow alike are ready for absolutely anything and keep quite calm until it happens. Waiting for something like that to come along, the farmer's principal concern is to negotiate the sale to bungalow builders of all the rough woodland he cannot be bothered to cultivate. And all this on subsidies! Each year his demands for help from the taxpayers are pushed through Parliament by city-bred legislators who *still* have romantic visions of Old Farmer Giles planting his seed corn in the south field when, in fact, he is closeted with his financial adviser discussing discounted cash flow and the return on capital employed.

The country dwellers have never had it so good; nor have the townsmen. Only the countryside suffers, the romantic, idyllic countryside. And as long as it is defended for what it is not by those who do not know it and exploited for what it is by those who do, it is likely to go on suffering for a very long time to come.

The gradual obliteration of the English countryside and the disappearance of every form of wild life is a melancholy prospect, although it would at least bring to an end, for want of subject matter, an argument that has divided the English for very many years. That is the Great

Fox Hunting Debate, in which both sides stick rigidly to untenable positions with an almost ritualistic obstinacy. The field sports abolitionists, the animal worshippers, stick to their anthropomorphic arguments ("How would I feel if I were a fox?") and refuse to recognize that foxes have to be killed, just as foxes have to kill. The fox-hunters announce that foxes are pests and that hunting is the best way of keeping them down. But that is not acceptable either, because everyone knows that the hunters do not go hunting from disinterested and unselfish service to the countryside. They do it for fun. That is what is wrong. It is not what hunting does to the foxes; it is what it does to the hunters. Not that the animal dies, but that people should want to kill it.

Of course, not all members of a hunt are full of blood-lust; they enjoy the chase for itself, the exhilaration of riding full-tilt across beautiful country on a frosty morning with the pack in full cry—and you must be blind or deaf not to sense that there *is* a profound exhilaration in these things. But something in them is dwarfed and stunted if this exhilaration is not outweighed by distaste that the end of all this should be killing for killing's sake, and what is dwarfed is humanity, and that fact cannot really be altered by the elegance and gentlemanliness of it all, or indeed by the elegance and gentlemanliness of what's written about it, for instance, an obituary like the farewell *The Times* bid recently to a well-known squire: "But, if he was a sage in business hours, he was always a boy at heart. The heart was given over to birds, beasts and flowers. He was an eager field naturalist and gardener, a still keener shot. And like most great English killers of birds, he was a merciful man who cherished the victims he slew so cleanly."

That is not really enough because if you are quoting what has been said about fox hunting, you have to go a little further, and quote the ex-officer who was recorded for the "Great War" series of programs. He said: "We were lying down in front of the canal at Mons when a Jerry appeared over the rise the other side. I said 'Right fire' to the private next to me: but he'd never actually fired at a man before and he couldn't bring himself to pull the trigger like that, in cold blood as it were. But I'd done quite a bit of hunting and shooting, and I was used to killing living things so I took aim and got him. I think that must have been the first German killed by the British Army."

In any case, arguments about fox hunting do at least take up time, which, according to all the people who ought to know, is beginning to hang a bit heavy. Like the rest of the western world, the English have lately discovered the problem of leisure (not that they would think for a moment of discussing it with others). For thousands of years, the problem has been to acquire some, but now the experts say there is a great change coming and within a few years there will be millions of people with time on their hands. The new problem is how to fill these terrifying hours and years of leisure. And it is not a bit of use telling the English to do what everyone else will do (take a good long holiday away from it all) because, as we have seen, they do not think much of short holidays away from it all, let alone long ones. In any case, it is not always possible, even briefly, to get away from it all. For example, according to one paper, a Mr. and Mrs. J. Easton of Norwich decided while they were on holiday in Southend to take a "mystery tour." The mystery tour took them to Norwich. They spent the day in the cattle market to avoid meeting friends. And when Miss Gertrude Usher went on a 1,300 mile week-end excursion by rail and steamer to the Inner Hebrides, she certainly got away for forty-eight hours, but still she thought her £5 and her time could have been better spent. "There was nothing but scenery up there," she said when she got back to Euston.

How, then, do the experts see the problem? First of all, not as one they will ever have to face themselves. The professional worriers, the new managerial aristocracy of the 20th century, do not expect any leisure. The successful people in industry and commerce and finance, in entertainment and journalism and politics and the professions and the universities—these people do not foresee any leisure at all. They expect to work harder and harder, handling ever bigger deals, solving ever knottier problems, turning ever faster bucks until they die. The pace of their lives makes quite impossible the enjoyment of leisure in the way that aristocrats of bygone days understood it. Their leisure was indeed leisurely. It involved the enjoyment of the slow passage of the seasons, the peaceful flow of nature, time for contemplation and reflection, the reading of long books at an easy pace, visits to friends lasting several months, a tour of Europe that included weeks on end in every important city.

The life of today's successful man is lived at a tempo which insures that if he has to spend fifteen minutes in a peaceful meadow he is twitching for something to do, and after three paragraphs of Gibbon he has to send the book to an assistant for a one-page summary.

The thing that worries these experts is not their leisure, but everyone else's. It is the prospect of a vast, underemployed proletariat which fills them with dread. Millions of people earning a good wage but only working a twenty-hour week is the nightmare of "responsible, far-seeing people" all over England. The solutions they propose are cultural and physical: educational television, pony trekking on Dartmoor, and outward-bound sea schools in our vibrant new national Gordonstoun.

But in fact, the desperately worried paternalists will probably not get their way. The dispossessed factory workers are not going to pole-vault their way into the 21st century. Unaware of the high-minded plans in store for them, they have already begun to find ways of using their leisure. A bit of it goes on the telly, and greyhound racing and bingo and similarly empty forms of time-passing indulged in by those lost souls who have not been given the grace to enjoy night clubs, horse racing and *chemin de fer*. But most of their leisure is spent working.

The tremendous boom in do-it-yourself of recent years is not just a criticism of England's interior decorators. It is the English thwarting, as only the English can, the devilish experts who would otherwise give them their idea of fun for idle hands to do. While the experts contemplate their schemes for perpetual self-improvement, masses of Englishmen spend their spare time painting ceilings, papering walls, filling their houses with cupboards and wardrobes and chests of drawers, installing copper plumbing and double-glazing, flooring the attic, and re-pointing the brickwork. Those tasks finished, they are underneath their cars, greasing and oiling them, improving performance and reducing consumption and generally tickling them up.

And, of course, there is plenty of work for a nation of gardeners, as a glance at the rising national expenditure on implements and requisites will show. Or a glance at the correspondence columns of the *Amateur Gardener*. "I wonder," wrote one man with time on his hands, even at the office, "if you could offer me some advice as to the type of plants which survive a hot, dry, dark atmosphere. Perhaps I should explain. I work in a large basement which has no window and consequently no natural daylight. I have to depend on a five-foot strip light which remains alight from only 9 A.M. till 5:30 P.M. each day. There are no external ventilators and the only means of obtaining any fresh air is either to leave the door open, or (for myself) to go and stand in the road for a while. If I leave the door open there is an excessive draft and therefore I must keep the fan-heater on all day, every day. I have had no success as yet in keeping and enjoying any form of plant life at all."

Well, other Englishmen are not so unlucky. They are enjoying fantastic success with their plant life and they have no leisure problems at all. Indeed, it is quite extraordinary the way a man will go on strike for better conditions at work, then go home and work for seven hours at a stretch, for no wage, in conditions that would have horrified Lord Shaftesbury. He builds a room extension into the garden and then a garden extension into the room extension and ends up eating the goldfish straight from the pool. In two years he has got a seven story bungalow with penthouse, garage and five bedrooms full of tropical fish. If everything else palls, he will build a brick wall, plaster it, and then stick on a wallpaper with a brick pattern.

Time does not hang quite so heavy after all. The English have solved their leisure "problem" on English soil without recourse to time-wasting holidays abroad. First by working like stink during every moment of leisure, and second by creating huge cases of leisure throughout the working day: this is done in factories by over-manning, feather-bedding, closed shops, demarcation rules, tea breaks and so on; bosses do the same thing by committee meetings, conference breakfasts, conference lunches, routine procedures, courses, seminars, and study groups. The end will surely be reached when every moment of leisure is spent at work and every moment of work is spent at leisure.

17

Le Sport
Le Weekend
and the
Haute Cuisine

IF THE English ever feel they are being a bit hard on foreigners—solving leisure problems in the way best calculated to exclude Continentals and the Continental way of doing things, and only spending time in those wretched countries in direct proportion to the amount of hardship and barbarism to be found there—there is one vital piece of evidence, one monumental example of foreign perversity, that they can fall back on. We gave them a chance. We really did. We entrusted to them perhaps the most valuable aspect of our leisure. We told them about sport. And look what they did to it.

The English invented sport. It is true that the Greeks had athletic tournaments, that medieval Europeans had jousts and tourneys, that the nobility all around the world have always found jolly ways of killing wild animals, and that Scotsmen have been throwing telegraph poles at each other since the dawn of time. Nevertheless, the concept of sport as organized open air competition of an essentially useless nature is an English one, and a recent English one at that. The word "sport" as we now use it did not occur until 1864—the idea is essentially Victorian. In particular the aura of decency and fair play and leisurely activity is Victorian, and the word sportsman as a term of praise is first recorded in 1893. The whole concept is so alien to other nations that the French, for example, have had to swipe the actual word from us (*Le sport*), since they cannot even translate it.

The essence of sport as the English have understood it is that it is not serious. It is a pleasant way of passing the time on golden summer afternoons, with the crack of leather on willow in an atmosphere of gentlemanliness, good fellowship and may-the-best-man-win. Indeed the final score is insignificant, and to be preoccupied with winning is itself unsportsmanlike, as Grantland Rice pointed out in his famous Victorian poem and fond uncles have inscribed in young nephews' autograph books ever since:

"For when the one Great Scorer comes
To write against your name.
He marks not that you won or lost,
But how you played the game."

However, once the benighted non-English got hold of sport, they set out deliberately to corrupt the whole ideal. It started with something very unworthy and shocking called professionalism, which meant that some cads actually received money for taking part in sport. Even worse, their rewards tended to be proportionate to the extent of their success—in other words, winning was of the first importance to them. By rights, this should have meant an end to all sport—since the essence of it had been that winning didn't matter. But sport did not end. It went on. It spread to more and more classes of people and more and more nations of the world. It became more and more organized, with huge international contests in Tokyo and Helsinki and Mexico City. It flooded the television screens of 500 million homes, and vast tracts of Swedish pine forests were felled so that the inhabitants of Ashton-under-Lyme could read the results of local football matches in New South Wales.

Then a terrible thing happened: English people started to accept money for participating in sports. Of course it was all secret, and everyone pretended it didn't happen unless the people were very poor. But worse was to follow—not as a result of professionalism, but in response to the discovery of violence. The casual and elegant pastime of the Empire-builders had become a focus for passion and punch-ups all around the globe. Boxing and wrestling were being pumped into millions of homes every day, and it wasn't Graeco-Roman wrestling or the elegant fisticuffs of Edwardian pugilists. The game of rugger turned into a mobile version of all-in wrestling, and by the middle of the 1960s the players were actually biting each other. They bit each other before that, of course, but the bitten had always been too gentlemanly to mention the fact.

Even cricket erupted into violence with chief interest centering on fast bowlers who might knock someone out (many of them were forced into throwing in order to wound the batsmen). In the West Indies, bottles were hurled at cricket players in a test match; in India, crowds rioted and one of the opposing batsmen had to flee to his hotel to escape the pursuit of an angry mob.

It was Association Football, however, which really caught on all round the world. The genial pastime of the Corinthian Casuals provided a battlefield for warring Koreans and Brazilians. In Latin America, passions broke out with stilettos and pistols, and referees went in fear of their lives. The Argentinians nearly turned the World Cup into a fight. Even in Britain, the annual Celtic Rangers match produced a few deaths and hundreds of injuries each year, spectators ripped railway trains to pieces, and the best-loved player in the land was the one most likely to give a slap across the chops to any opponent who got in his way.

If the English found the rise of professionalism un-gentlemanly, they found the rise of violence unspeakable. To try to win for money was bad enough, but to resort to illegal and violent means to achieve it was beneath contempt. The only visible result, however, was a further rise in the popularity of football all round the world. Why? It seems clear now that the trouble with the world over the last 20 years has been a surfeit of peace and altogether too little violence and danger for the satisfaction of those who go in for that sort of thing. Into a world with insufficient available violence, football came like the answer to a prayer. Some can play and expend the violence directly, the rest can watch and expend it vicariously. The parallel with ancient Rome may be obvious, but it is none the less significant. In the days of the Republic and the citizen army, when every man might have to fight for his country and his life, there was no colisseum. In the days of the Empire, when there was a professional army, more wealth and leisure, and no fighting, the gladiatorial arena was evolved to satisfy the craving for violence of those who had no other outlet. They had bread and circuses, we have football and fish fingers.

But this appalling new creature the foreigners have created out of our sport does more than siphon off surplus violence. It also provides a non-military focus for nationalism. The Olympic Games and the World Cup and the European Cup Winners' Cup and a host of other international events have provided a comparatively harmless outlet for national rivalry and national pride. Moreover, there are so many different sports that almost every nation can be best at something. And they do all like to win. In the old days we let them join in but it was our game, so naturally—although it did not matter who won—we won. But now there is no doubt that these violent sporting contests do provide an antidote to the inflammatory function of the United Nations, where people say such nasty things to each other. Of all the stupid ideas current in the world at this moment, the most dangerous is that we should keep politics out of sport. On the contrary, we must keep politics in sport—we let it out at our peril. Athletic nationalism seems to be the best insurance we have.

You can see the real reason why South Africa excludes mixed sport. It is not because the social mixing would do any harm—if they played against colored teams, the colored team might win, and this would be a victory for African nationalism. Equally, you can see the folly of it. It denies the Africans an outlet, it inhibits their chance of evolving national heroes and salving their pride. Their only way is by political movements and conspiracy against the state. Already, in the rest of the Negro world, the real heroes are not Martin Luther King or Albert Luthuli: they are Cassius Clay—who identified his sporting success with nationalism by joining the black Muslims—Sobers, the West Indian cricketer, and Eusebio, the Portuguese football player. Better that than another Attila or Chahka or Genghis Khan.

There is one nation which more than any other is a danger politically and militarily to the peace and continued existence of the others, namely China. Some people think that we must at all costs get her admitted to the United

Nations. That really would put the cap on it. Russia's membership in the United Nations did nothing for world peace in Stalin's time. To an Englishman reared on the English way of sport it seems potty of course, but it was when athletic contests started, when Communist heroes like Zatopek and Kuts gained their triumphant victories over capitalist athletes, when the Hungarian footballers and the Moscow Dynamos started teaching the West a lesson, that tension began to ease off. The root of all our present troubles is clearly that never since World War II have the Chinese competed in the Olympics or the World Cup. They have never met us in athletic combat. Therefore they feel that the only way to triumph over us is by military strength. Obviously, we must forget the United Nations: China must be admitted to the Olympic Games and the World Cup. A few punch-ups between Nobby Stiles and Ping Ho at Wembley, a few bottles hurled onto the pitch at Canton, mutual allegations of cheating and sharp practice in the next Pentathlon, and the future peace of the world will be on a sounder footing than it has been at any time this century.

Unfortunately, this will not be enough for the foreigners. To have taken our national pastime and turned it into the battlefield to end all battlefields will not be enough. They will still go on wanting to come over here and wreak their ghastly havoc upon us in the flesh. And that, of course, we can't have. We know that foreigners have been submitted to a good deal of unpleasantness in their own countries in recent years, poor things. The English have certain traditions, we know—no other nation in the world combines such a reputation for hospitality to those in need with such public unanimity about the need for harsher immigration laws—but we really cannot have them all here. We quite realize that immigrants come to this country because they find their own frightful for some reason or other and cherish the deeply-felt ambition to move to England. But don't they realize that it is not just them? That all round the world *everybody* feels like that? We just have to say "No" these days to more or less everyone from abroad.

With one exception. If they want to serve us food. That is the one loophole. We resent foreign customs, we dislike foreign manners, we find almost all forms of foreign influence distasteful, but if they want to serve us food, it's different. The "serving" part is important. It's the "service" aspect that makes it possible for us to accept the idea. And then it's the "food" bit that clinches it.

It would not always have been so. Once upon a time food in England was abysmal, and foreign influence upon it would have been as unwelcome then as it is upon almost everything else now. We have always felt that there was some correlation between our sterling qualities and our appalling food. For a hundred years, the abysmal boarding school diet sent out clean-limbed, clear-eyed young Englishmen to deal with lesser breeds without the law. The Battle of Britain was won on the dining tables of Repton. *Haute cuisine* was for effete foreigners, hysterically obsessed with inessentials, like sex. France had Escoffier, England had King Alfred. For us, food was leathery meat, watery greens, leaden suet puddings, stewed tea, pink blanc mange, and tapioca. It was epitomized by the seaside boarding house waitress bending over a customer with the magic words "Gravy, sir. One lump or two?"

Then suddenly there was a change. It came in the mid-fifties, around the time of Suez. In the past hundred years, our international stature and our dreary food had seemed two sides of the same coin. When the glory departed with Suez, so did the need to eat the uneatable. Perhaps since the others ate better and also fared better, there was even a direct relationship instead of an inverse one: perhaps the availability of good meals was an incentive to earn more money to afford them. Besides, what was the harm in having a few of these foreign types over here to cook for us or wait on us? After all, we already had dreadful regional dishes like tripe, lavabread, and haggis. Why not go a bit further afield for our regions?

Of course, this was not going on in isolation. Already one extremely attractive invasion had begun. It can be summed up in one word—Capucino. And with it, Italian coffee houses, decorated with taste and imagination, unlike the lugubrious native establishments, and serving excellent coffee as well as strange but exciting dishes like gnocchi, ravioli, and spaghetti (the latter slightly spoiled by the quaint but forgivable Italian habit of forgetting to put a slice of toast under it). These cafes started in London, but quite soon they spread—without nationalist opposition—until they covered the country.

The Italians were closely followed by the Chinese, with their habits—both novel to our own caterers—of serving their food hot, then *keeping* it hot at the table with little candles. Goodness, how odd! But also how delicious! Apart from their implacable indifference to a good cup of tea, choosing instead to serve us little sips of wishy-washy liquid, without milk, in cups without handles, we found no fault with the Chinese and it was not long before every suburb was furnished with a cheap and cheerful Chinese restaurant.

Next came *haute cuisine,* which arrived in force. Though its march was irresistible, there were odd pockets of resistance: Some diners sent back steak *tartare* with the angry complaint that it hadn't been cooked and consommé Julienne because it was cold; other puzzled customers asked bewilderedly why it was that Gruyère cheese had the holes in when it was Gorgonzola that needed the ventilation. But in general, *haute cuisine* was welcomed by everybody. The Greeks, Spaniards, and Hungarians followed the French, and by 1966, Soho stretched from Lands End to John O'Groats—and the Good Food Club had increased its membership in fifteen years from 8,000 to more than 100,000 with a similarly phenomenal rise in the number of places where good food was actually available.

Even the Americans were welcome. They brought with them a new literary style. As we read the menus they prepared we learned that "Rich succulent farm-fresh dawn-gathered dew-drenched sun-kissed" meant "Frozen." That "From the garden of England royal King Edward potatoes dug from the rich soil of Kent and deep-fried in sizzling olive oil" meant "chips." And that "A tangy elusive vanilla sauce, the secret centuries-old recipe of hooded monks" was "custard." Chicken Maryland, broiler chicken spit-roasted in the window, corn-on-the-cob, and waffles arrived in force. We were even prepared to go into their Wimpy bars and use that language they have so skilfully chosen to make you feel totally inferior. After all, once you have been forced to say " I would like a chocolate Whipsy with a giant economy burger" your dignity has gone forever—and any pretense of being a major maritime power along with it.

In supermarkets, decidedly un-English commodities like Chinese mushrooms and frozen paella jostled for space with Ambrosia Creamed Rice Pudding. Restaurants all over the country were being given names like "Escargot," but no one was opening establishments named after good, solid English dishes. No one was saying "Wine and dine at the Fresh Cabbage." "Meet your friends at the Bread Pudding." Or, "After the theatre why not rendezvous at the Stewed Prune?" (One foreign verb even infiltrated itself into that last sentence.)

Meanwhile Britain's new breed of gastronomes (it is almost impossible to avoid the word "gourmet") are being sent, like explorers, farther and farther afield in their search for the Valhalla of cuisine. Once it was *sole Goujon* in a little-known cafe in Lyons. Now it's kous-kous on palm leaves in a Marrakesh market place. Any day now we can expect to see Robert Carrier of the *Sunday Times* come staggering out of a tent at the South Pole and wandering out into the blizzard because there is only enough penguin à l'orange for three persons . . . or food expert Egon Ronay returning from a tour of darkest Africa with news of an offbeat Swahili bistro where the specialty of the house is food expert Raymond Postgate.

Clearly the *Times* will never again have occasion, as it did a few years ago, to publish this sort of letter: "The thirtieth annual Foire Gastronomique, perhaps the greatest food fair in Europe, has just ended here in Dijon. The British stand (a poor thing, but our own) was displaying, among other national delicacies, tins of cat and dog food."

Mind you, we have not surrendered totally to the foreigners. We are doing our best to make them English— or at least credit the English. When the British Travel and Holiday Association boasts of English cooking as the best in the world, what it means is that our Indian, Chinese, Italian and French restaurants are as good as any you will find anywhere. And the Anglicizing has become subtle indeed. One rooftop restaurant in London prints the English description of a dish in heavy type, and the French description underneath. When you get to the end of the meal the menu offers as dessert the well-known English "petit fours." Underneath is the translation into French: "Les frivolités Françaises."

18

The
White Man's
Burden

THE English, as we have seen, cherish any number of illusions. But there is one Grand Illusion. Among many illogicalities, one breach of logic towers over all. One subject which contains within it an infinite number of the oddities and perversities we have been talking about: the attitude toward Public Money as opposed to the public's money, the irresistible growth of innumerable official departments, the curious stratifications the English seem prepared to accept within their society, the quixotic blend of mistrust and superiority they feel when considering any other society, the questions they are apparently not expected to ask, the dubious truths they are clearly expected to welcome, and even the substitutes for religion that, one way or another, they yearn to discover.

They all come together on one bill for £2,000,000,000 a year, under one heading—Defense. The price the English pay for their army, navy, and air force. These days there may not be many horses left to guard, colors to troop, or households to be cavalry for, but that is the bill. £2,000,-000,000 a year. The price they pay for the army, the navy, and the air force is the price they pay for peace and security. If they did not pay, the Russians would be marching through Muswell Hill in no time.

The price is absolutely fantastic, of course—more than twenty times what is spent on roads or hospitals. As a simple sum it may not sound a great deal in American terms. But to the English it is a staggering burden. Not just because England is a smaller country, with proportionately smaller spending power. But because her proportionately smaller expenditure on defense is for a quite disproportionately smaller purpose. At least the American Taxpayer can feel as he gazes at mounting defense costs that perhaps he is maintaining some sort of world status quo, that perhaps this is some sort of world competition that it is impossible for him to opt out of. But to the English Taxpayer, as he gazes at *his* mounting defense costs, there is no such consolation. He knows that he is maintaining no status quo, that far from being irretrievably committed to some world competition in armed power, he is often not even selected as umpire any more. The folly of this sort of military thinking is universal, but it is the English who have chosen to incarnate this folly.

The sum they spend adds up to between a third and a

half of the total sum that the Government spends on *every-thing*. The sum is so incredibly huge that (a) nobody can understand how much it is and (b) nobody can believe that such a vast sum could be spent without the nation's getting value for it, or at least for most of it. Certainly no one can believe that nine-tenths of it is wasted, even though this is the case.

It is impossible to tot up the profit and loss account of Defense expenditure. The English pour this £2,000,-000,000 every year into the services, and what do they get out of it? Peace and security are the only answers. But it's like advertising and PR—how do you know you wouldn't have done just as well without it? How do you know that without this vast defense expenditure England wouldn't have just as much peace and security as she has now?

If we were conquering territory, protecting and developing markets for our produce, insuring by military means an ample cheap supply of raw materials for our industries, then we would have some practical justification for the Services who did all this, even if it attracted the moral obloquy of the world. But we do not do this: defense *per se* is all we are concerned with. The aircraft carriers, the atomic submarines, the fighters and V-bombers, the missiles and the anti-missile missiles, the complicated electronic ranging and guidance and tracking systems, Bloodhound and Sea Slug and Blue Streak and Blue Water and Polaris and TSR-2 and F-111—they all exist only to defend us for as long as they are able. The R.A.F., for instance, now has a plane that can get halfway to Russia before it becomes obsolete.

But what therefore are they all defending us *against?* The absurd part of the whole game is that if anyone wants to eliminate this country, they are free to do so any time they choose. Already there are several hundred pieces of hardware orbiting in the stratosphere which no one pays any attention to. Fifty of these could be H-bomb warheads capable of being directed onto our biggest cities. Equally, H-bomb components could easily be smuggled into the country separately and assembled in private houses in city centers ready for detonation at short notice. There are several poisons of such deadly concentration that a few bottles in twenty reservoirs could solve our population problem for ever. There are bacteria which could be released in the atmosphere. Against none of these have we any defense whatever, nor do we seek any. Since England's enemies have not destroyed us by these methods, we have to fall back on the militarily incredible assumption that they do not want to.

If you look at the question of what the Services are for from the point of view of the nation's real needs, you will find no answer. You must look at it from the point of view of the needs of the services, the need to continue and if possible grow larger, irrespective of objective values. There was a time after World War II when it seemed— and arguably was—necessary for nations to acquire nuclear bombs, to construct the "balance of terror." However, a stage was reached in the fifties when both sides had the power to eliminate each other, and defense against elimination became even more obviously impossible. The vast, multi-million dollar DEW line warned the USA of rockets approaching from the USSR—provided the Russians had the grace to send them over the north polar route. Before the line was operational, the Russians had the capacity to send the rockets over the South Pole. By then it was clear that the technology of destruction would always be years ahead of the technology of interception, and both sides gave up hope of real defense.

This posed a dilemma. If defense was impossible, and both sides had all the weapons of destruction they could use, why continue to have an army or a navy or an air force? Why not keep a few men in underground blockhouses with radar screens, hot-lines and buttons, and release the rest for gainful employment? The Services needed to think very hard to answer that, and with great skill and enterprise they evolved an entirely new defense philosophy. All through history, soldiers have chosen military resources to combat existing dangers and threats. Now for the first time they reversed the process; they chose military dangers and threats to fit existing military resources. If they had anti-aircraft missiles, the danger was hostile aircraft-carrying bombs. If they had foreign bases and 150,000 soldiers, the danger was small hostile operations on the ground by non-nuclear nations. If they had bombers with a 2,000-mile range, the danger was reprisal-worthy attacks by powers within 2,000 miles of our bomber bases. All other dangers could be ignored, indeed had to be ignored, since they were without visible remedies. There are many hostile aggressions and dangers to peace in areas around the globe where Britain has no troops and no jurisdiction; that's just too bad, we can't do anything about it. If Mao attacks Tibet or the whole of the Middle East is involved in war we can only sigh. But if there is guerrilla activity in Aden or Borneo, it is a threat to peace which Britain must deal with or the whole world will go up in flames.

It seems necessary to spend a great deal of money recruiting soldiers in view of the way English spheres of influence have been decreasing. (As one R.A.F. colonel said, "There's not much pink on the old map any more." And he was looking at the map of England.) Recruitment is indeed an elaborate confidence trick, suggesting a life of shirtsleeves and sunlight and complex technical equipment, and instead providing months of basic draining followed by years of boredom overseas, with Military Police coming to fetch them back in handcuffs after the three years are up. And yet they are vital. When people suggest that the whole of our Defense should be handed over to civilian scientists and managers who would obviously manage it a great deal better, the Service chiefs have only one answer: "Ah, but they could not handle men out in the field." So the Service chiefs must have men out in the field. Not so much to protect the country as to protect themselves.

Those stupid patrol skirmishes in which privates get

killed defending territories we are due to leave in a year or two anyway are the only justification for all the majors and colonels and generals and admirals who clutter up Whitehall and Bath. Navy chiefs try valiantly to insist that not everyone in the Navy is obsessed with the idea of somehow infiltrating back into the comforts of the Admiralty: a recent census showed that only 27% of men serving in the Navy wanted to be admirals—but these figures, while impressive, were somewhat invalidated by the fact that the other 73% are admirals already.

Whenever we hear from some far-flung corner of the globe that "Guerrilla forces today launched a series of attacks on Government bases," we know with sinking heart that they mean "Democrats are trying to overthrow our Fascist puppet" and that before long, more English soldiers will be pitchforked into the whole pointless exercise to die, be injured, or simply to rot for a cause which is irrelevant to English democracy, and quite probably inimical to theirs. And yet it must be so.

Otherwise the whole business could be divided up between the skills of civilians and the decisions of politicians. So there have to be men. About 10 years ago it was said England was not safe without a minimum army of 180,000; they only got 158,000 so the dangers were scaled down to fit the reduced size and we haven't felt the draft. It could have been 50,000 except that that would have brought the country closer and closer to a situation in which one single patrol in Malaya would be the justification for fifty generals, five hundred colonels, and five thousand majors.

Trooping the color, horse guards and all the rest of the pageantry play a vital part in keeping up the illusion. Clearly, no manager in an automobile factory could drill *his* men into moving with precision and unison, and indeed the men would be far too sensible to cooperate if he tried. So we can all see on ceremonial occasions that there is some mystique in operation, something unique the military can do and civilians can't do, thereby concealing the fact that virtually all their other operations could be better done by engineers, mathematicians, shipping and air lines (with the possible exception of BEA) clerks, electricians, truck drivers, managers, and the rest of the civilian community.

The justification offered by those too realistic to pretend that we get any real defense for the money is that it does a great deal for industry. This, of course, is utter twaddle. If the sums spent on the Services were released for industrial research, development, and expansion they would do thousands of times more good. Huge amounts are purchased from the U.S.A.—Polaris missiles and the F-111 are only the top of the iceberg. Our overseas garrisons are a desperate drain on our foreign exchange. The Services were letting the British computer industry die, and it was the civilian Ministry of Technology that saved it. Our machine tool industry was not saved from appalling decline by the Services, and the result of their impact on the aircraft industry was that the U.S. got the swing wing,

THE WHITE MAN'S BURDEN

and we had to embark on an abortive Anglo-French civil aircraft project in an attempt to rescue it from the extinction threatened by years of hesitation and muddle. Our really promising projects like hover-craft and civilian atomic energy and de-salination plants and executive jets owe little or nothing to the Services and could have benefited tremendously from one percent of the annual defense budget. Only the combined strength of the Army Act and the Official Secrets Act prevent the nation from knowing just how many of its present troubles spring from that annual £2,000,000,000 of which the majority goes down the drain. What is clear is that it would certainly be a great deal more useful to give every man, woman and child in this country £40, and tell them to defend themselves.

So why does the nation tolerate the whole extraordinary mess? Partially, the answer is in looking at the medieval village churches and the great gothic cathedrals all over Europe, and instead of admiring their unquestioned beauty, ask yourself the more mundane question, "Where did the money come from?" After all, there was little enough surplus cash in the thirteenth and fourteenth centuries, and yet even with today's mechanized and automated techniques it would cost millions of pounds to build a cathedral like Chartres, or Lincoln.

The answer is that fear about the future is embedded deep in the nature of man, and anyone who can make him believe that by the expenditure of money he can remove the need for fear can make his fortune. Medieval man believed that by sinking labor and time and wealth into churches and cathedrals he could insure for himself peace and safety after death. The belief was illogical, the hope was an illusion, and the product was a wasteful use of much-needed resources, but it was the best-looking chance of salvation, so it was taken.

Modern man believes that by sinking labor and time and wealth into atomic submarines and rockets and aircraft carriers and weapons system he can insure for himself peace and security before death. The belief is illogical, the hope is an illusion, and it is a wasteful use of much-needed resources, but it is the best-looking chance of salvation and so it, too, is taken.

Radar systems and rocket ranges may not, to our eyes, rival Lincoln or Chartres, but future generations will be able to read the same lesson from both. It is perhaps fanciful to pursue the parallel further and see the three services as three monastic orders, the khaki friars, the dark blue friars, and the light blue friars. But—they live off the rest of us because we believe in their illusory mystic power to protect us; they own their own property, which cannot be disposed of as easily as civil property; their lower orders live lives of disciplined rigor and the senior ones enjoy considerable luxury; it is difficult to leave once you have joined; and they are tried by their own courts and not by the laws of the land. Admittedly, some soldiers are not very monastic in their behavior, but then neither were the monks.

It does sometimes seem that the fighting services are moving toward a state in which they do no fighting at all, but this is not quite true. Some of the most terrible battles of modern times have been fought out at Whitehall, between the Navy and the R.A.F. for aircraft; between the R.A.F. and the Army for weapons systems; and between all three and the Cabinet to resist demands for contraction, economy, and integration. A short paragraph in the *London Gazette* noting the retirement of a general or an admiral may not match the name on the war memorial, but it often betokens a battle fought with equal passion and endurance and will to survive. Little skirmishes in Aden and Sarawak are only distractions: even if peace reigns throughout the world, the Whitehall warriors will fight on.

£2,000,000,000 a year does seem an awful lot to pay for a few splendid pageants, several extra departments, a papier-mâché tribal totem-pole, and for keeping a large group of admirals and generals from gainful employment as cinema commissionaires.

The system has disadvantages in addition to the cost. The officer-other rank idea perpetuates class attitudes in society. It permeates and bedevils relationships between the manager class and their employees, whom they subconsciously expect to leap to obey every command—as the troops did when they were in the army. Not to mention the havoc caused by the retired army officer, rank of captain and above, who, long after discarding his uniform, continues to use his Army rank to put the fear of God into his domestic staff, kindle passionate aspirations in the bosom of the sub-postmistress and the district nurse, and make the grocer think twice before mentioning a long overdue bill.

The organization of the Army, with Corps and Division and Brigade and Battalion, is the pattern for the worst kind of bureaucracy, followed slavishly and fatally by all too many non-military institutions. It insures England a large body of senior and authoritative citizens very close to the seat of power who have a vested interest in making peaceful situations appear tense, tense ones dangerous, and dangerous ones explosive, and whose lucrative defense contracts make many others outside Whitehall all too anxious to support their warnings. It is the sort of pressure of which MP's who represent constituencies with large armaments factories are only too aware. One such MP, addressing a meeting during the last election, said, "My party will continue to work for peace." At this he heard a certain amount of muttering so he added quickly, "But not in our time, of course."

The system contrives, too, to release each year from the Services into society thousands of young men trained in the use of weapons and unarmed combat and prepared for and perhaps experienced in the use of violence—not only those who were made to face violence for the first time but also those who joined for the very wish to face it. In the words of the commercial the Services have never shown on television, "I did not join the Army to learn a

trade or to see the world. I joined the Army to kill people."
Obviously, every single one of them is not likely to be
obsessed with violence, but there can be few without the
habit of shouting at their subordinates, obeying their superiors without thought or question, and conforming totally
to the behavior and standards of those around them.

There is no doubt that a time in the military can
inculcate a whole new set of values, as was demonstrated
by the general who told the *Daily Express,* "It will probably be four or five years before either the Russians or the
Americans have accumulated a sufficient stock of missiles
with a range of 5,000 miles. To start a war with anything
less than this would be folly. . . ." Incredible logic.

When you have discussed all the minimal advantages
of defense, and all the assorted disadvantages, you come
back to that one baleful fact: that the problems of home-
lessness, understaffed schools and hospitals, crowded roads,
colander jails, and the rest of it, come down to shortage
of money—money which is poured into the Services to
pay that £2,000,000,000 bill. For that is the key to the
English delusion. The English simply cannot afford it. The
Americans incredibly seem to have the sort of economy
that can absorb a full-scale war in Asia almost as a matter
of course. The English economy starts to totter if there's
a Seamen's Strike.

If Government is concerned with the creation of
wealth, Politics is concerned with its distribution. If wealth
is the ability to have the things you enjoy having or need,

why are the English squandering all this on what they neither need nor enjoy having, in order to make themselves literally "poor"? They are crippling themselves by refusing to opt out of a military power business from which everyone else seems to know they are—for all practical purposes—already excluded. The logic of being in Borneo and Sarawak, and not in Java, is becoming increasingly difficult to maintain. Ten years ago, Suez was England's affair: this last time, it wasn't. At the moment, Aden seems to be. But in ten years time?

England is immeasurably the best place in the world to live. Its people are more tolerant and more talented than even they believe. It has a uniquely important part to play in the modern world. What Athens was in the Roman Empire, England can and should be in the American Empire of the 1970's. Indeed, perhaps a small start has already been made, as the flow of Greek tutors to Rome is paralleled by the flow of English nannies to New York. From all over the Roman Empire, men journeyed to Athens. The Athenians knew something about the art of living that their visitors were only beginning to learn. The Athenians themselves had once been a great imperial power, but now what their history seemed to give them was roots, taste, a tradition for civilized art. There was a decency and a common sense, even an elegance and a wisdom. The influence, authority, even power, that Athens had in the development of that Empire in which they were militarily so insignificant is incalculable. It was an intellectual grandeur greater than any minute or momentary military grandeur that could have been gained from an attempt to rival Rome in an area in which Rome was unquestionably dominant.

England has all the qualifications to play the role of Athens. Why on earth then does she insist on crippling herself without point or purpose by trying to be a mini-Rome?